British Comedy *Greats*

British Comedy *Greats*

Introduction by Miles Kington

Edited by Annabel Merullo and Neil Wenborn

 CASSELL
ILLUSTRATED

Contents

Introduction
Miles Kington

There is a theory that humour is international and joins nations together, a theory held mainly by those who have little sense of humour and haven't travelled much. You only have to cross to France, look at the huge posters of French comic stars beside the road and fail to recognise any of them to realise that not only does comedy not travel very well, it doesn't even travel twenty-two miles across the Channel. How many people in Britain, for instance, remember the French comedian Coluche? Yet not many years ago he was so popular in France that he even ran for the presidency against Pompidou, and was given a fair chance of doing well. (His slogan: 'If you have to have a comedian in the Élysée Palace, why not get a genuine one?'…)

Similarly, the comic landmarks in the memory of anyone who grew up in Britain will be instantly recognisable to most other British people, and unknown abroad. Yes, there are exceptions. Yes, there are Benny Hill and Mr Bean, who have won global fame (and they are punished for it by not being included in this book!).

But although we tend to think that, for instance, Morecambe and Wise were one of the funniest comic duos of all time, the rest of the world has had to evolve in ignorance of them. In the year 2002 there was a hit on the West End stage called *The Play What I Wrote*, which was a tribute to Eric and Ernie written and acted by Sean Foley and Hamish McColl. It transferred to Broadway in early 2003, but as nobody in New York was familiar with the *oeuvre* of Eric and Ernie *all references to them were deleted from the show*, which is a bit like removing all allusions to Scotland from a touring production of *Macbeth*, just in case.

Well, I have news for the experts on Broadway. In December 2002 my wife and I took our fifteen-year-old son to London to see *The Play What I Wrote*, and he thought it was one of the funniest things he had ever seen in his life, even though he too had never heard of or seen Morecambe and Wise. Everything came through – the relationship, the jokes, the catchphrases, the business, even the star guest. The night we went the star guest was Twiggy. She was very good and funny. He had never heard of her either.

But for me the show set off a thousand little bells of memory, based on past years of rushing to the TV to watch the two. This despite the fact that I would be hard pushed to quote anything from all the Eric and Ernie shows I watched. Similarly, when I read Christopher Dunkley's essay on Morecambe and Wise in this book, and came across the line given to Glenda Jackson in one of those Shakespearean cameos forced on guest stars ('*Glenda/Cleopatra*: All men are fools and what makes them so is having beauty like what I have got'), I found myself hooting out loud with laughter. It wasn't so much the actual line. It wasn't the memory of it (I didn't remember it). It was the way the one bit of phrasing brought back the whole world of Morecambe and Wise, a memory which, dormant most of the time, is still so potent when aroused.

That's what this book is all about. It is a guilt-free memory trip, in which the patient can be laid back on the couch and asked to free-associate, not about their parents but about the lost joys of their earlier life. Recall will come flooding back. (As I approached the Hancock essay, I could suddenly hear from nowhere his voice saying: 'Does the name of Magna Carta mean nothing to you? Did she die in vain?') As if you were being done on *This Is Your Life*, the curtains will open and old familiar TV shows and radio sounds will come out to greet you, and remind you how you grew up together.

Or even how you grew up with them through your children. My two eldest children are now in their thirties, and if it had not been for them I would never have fallen in love with *The Young Ones* over their shoulder – a show not totally unlike the radio *Hancock's Half-Hour* in a way, in that four disparate but equally loony characters were condemned to live together in the same house for no discernible reason. And the first TV show that my fifteen-year-old son fell in love with twenty years later was – anyone? No, it was *The Young Ones* as well, on the scratchy old videos I had saved for two decades. Twenty years on, and just as effective.

Then he moved on to *Blackadder* and I followed him, and then on to *Father Ted* and I followed him. And one day all these comedy memories will be found lurking in his psyche, making him the British cultural exemplar he is – and not so very different from those of other ages either. He thinks, for instance, that the *Blackadder* team were the first people to have the brilliant idea of making fun of history. But, as Sarah Gristwood's essay here reminds us, it's been around for two hundred years at least. One of Jane Austen's shorter, less remembered but funniest books is *The History of England by a Partial, Prejudiced, and Ignorant Historian*. Then there was a Victorian *Punch* writer called Gilbert à Beckett who wrote a *Comic History of England*. And there were Sellar and Yeatman with *1066 and All That*, which I grew up with.

And in the 1960s Terry Jones and Michael Palin did a quite unjustly forgotten TV show called *The Complete and Utter History of Britain*. (I can still remember one scene from the era of the Battle of Hastings. An Anglo-Saxon is manning a stall with a placard saying 'A Year to Remember! – Get Your Souvenirs!', and he has thousands of unsold mugs labelled '1065'. 'Yes,' the stall holder is saying. 'Didn't quite get the product right, I'm afraid…')

You won't find that programme commemorated in this book, for the very good reason that the whole thing, I believe, was totally wiped by an enlightened TV company. But you'll find pretty much everything else lodged in your memory bank. Not quite everything. There are one or two things which I rather wished the editors had included myself. But that's one of the great things about the book, they told me. It'll get people arguing. Get people debating what should have been put in and left out. If we put everything in a book, then people can't have fun arguing about the omissions, can they?

Well, they've got pretty damn near everything, and reading the book has caused me to suffer a memory flood in which I damn near drowned, so I urge you to take it gently, a bit at a time, nice and easy does it… You won't, of course. But don't say I didn't warn you.

Absolutely Fabulous
Chrissy Iley

When *Absolutely Fabulous* crashed onto our screens in 1992 it was so exhilarating it was almost hallucinogenic. Like all satires – and that's essentially what it is – it punctured the prevailing orthodoxy, in this case the onset of dreary political correctness; it blasted the aura of the grey John Major years and then went on heartily to mock the piety and self-righteousness of Tony Blair long before most of the rest of the world knew he was going to make so many references to God.

Patsy and Edina began life as a French and Saunders sketch, but they were always larger than that. Joanna Lumley pre-Patsy was marbles-in-the-mouth posh totty. Elegant, straight. As the champagne-guzzling, wake-up-with-fag-in-her-mouth fashion director who got her job because she slept with the publisher, she sent herself up deliciously and became a new kind of fantasy. She showed what men could only have dreamt was on the inside, something very dirty. Jennifer Saunders' Eddy is an immaculately observed comic creation of that Nineties species the PR guru, who wants to save the dolphins and chant for fame and money – and for Kate Moss to do her fashion show. The characters demanded bigger screen time and a vaster audience. This was obviously too good for a one-off: it captured the moment, pushed it in our face and made it last forever.

Absolutely Fabulous has never been about convoluted plot twists. It's about the characters themselves. Whole episodes can be dedicated to Edina's fat trauma or to Patsy's sluttish Sixties beauty that segued into the nonstop Bolly of the Nineties and the new millennium. They are adorable because they refuse to grow up, refuse to be responsible. They are intoxicatingly selfish, yet loyal to each other by default.

The backdrop spans three generations of women. The younger generation is represented by the prim daughter Saffy (played by Julia Sawalha), who has rebelled against her liberated mother. She remains in her buttoned-up cardigan, with her buttoned-up loyalty to Blairism and all things prim and proper. She is the polar opposite of her mother, but has much more in common with her dotty grandmother (played by June Whitfield), who is a strange conglomeration of the other two characters. Her attitudes are more relaxed than Saffy's, but can be as harsh and selfish as Eddy's in an old-person, 'I'm-not-really-with-it' way.

Although the humour was so very much about capturing the *Zeitgeist*, somehow what's really funny about it doesn't date, even when you look at early episodes of Eddy calling from her thick-as-a-brick mobile outside her office to say 'I'm entering the building now'. The phone might be old, but the character's voice isn't. A few hip buzzwords might have changed, and Marni and Marc Jacobs might have replaced Lacroix, but her unrivalled

---

Women behaving badly: Patsy (Joanna Lumley) and Eddy (Jennifer Saunders)

greed, selfishness and vulnerability, all vying for attention, still make her enthralling.

Patsy and Eddy were prototypes of many things. For a start, they were the incarnation of women behaving badly. They were drunk, out on the town and out of it, and attracting the attention of bad boys and idiots, long before Zoë Ball and crew started spending evenings in the Met Bar with a few pints. They were fantastic role-models, because they did everything wrong and survived. Neither of them ever seemed to work, but irritatingly they always pulled things off. They were funny because they provided a vicarious thrill. Who wouldn't want to be vain, arrogant, obsessed with fat and fashion, and not only get away with it, but get away with it while hanging out with all the celebrities and hot labels of the moment? It's about our dual relationship with fame. We're all in thrall to it and we all want to despise it. Patsy and Edina made you think you could be right there. They shared with you what it was like to be in with the cutting-edge crew and made it all seem exciting, pathetic and ridiculous at the same time.

The character of Eddy is notoriously based on PR guru Lynne Franks, with whom Jennifer Saunders and script editor Ruby Wax are friends. Yes, friends. What they got from her was how she could unashamedly marry chanting spirituality with getting-you accounts. Being a new age hippie and a self-focusing PR guru seemed incongruous, but that's what she embraced, the having it all. None of this was done with harshness. It was done with affection.

Lynne Franks herself is larger than life, and was a metaphor for the nice Nineties that had come out of the greedy Eighties. She was and is outrageous. Many times I've been with her and had strictly *Absolutely Fabulous* moments. When we were both living in LA, she decided to embrace me. Before long, I had the run of her address book. At nine o'clock I could have Selena the Goddess-builder rework my bum, followed by a stone massage by a man from Hawaii who was going to make me grow two inches. Then I might have my aura exchanged by a woman dressed head to toe in white. In the evening Lynne might come to a party I was throwing where she'd offered to bring the food, but invariably she'd eat it all in the car before she got there and arrive with a bag of greasy bones from Koo Koo Roo. Realising that she was flawed, she'd then turn up with flowers or a present the next day. It's precisely that sweetness and selfishness that Eddy embodies, and that makes her human and one of us. She is a person we all dread and would love to be, and a person who is in all of us.

Patsy, far from being an anachronism, has grown into herself. In an era that's got more and more moral, restrained and tight-lipped – we're not even supposed to eat wheat now – her outrageousness is so refreshing it's liberating. How fantastic that somebody drinks more champagne than we do. I can't look at a bottle of Bolly without thinking of Patsy. Bolly is the straight-to-the-point, no-subtlety champagne. It does the job. She's almost like Eddy's surrogate daughter, which makes the dynamic with Eddy's real daughter even more piquant. Saffy is so censorious, non-smoking and organic fleece-wearing. By the fourth series, she has become increasingly concerned about globalisation and pension plans, and she hero worships Cherie Blair. She has been able to grow up with the times. She started off as a naïve sixteen-year-old. Now she's even more ridiculously amusing as a naïve twenty-four-year-old.

All three generations of women embody neuroses and insecurities of femaleness. *Ab Fab* is probably the first ever female-centric comedy that is not just available and funny for women. It's not easy for women to be laughed at. To be laughed at is somehow humiliating, and pre-*Ab Fab* it was impossible for a woman to be sexy and funny at the same time. Yet certainly Patsy retains her full-on sluttiness as a poster girl, and the part has given Joanna Lumley's own career a new lease of life. There could be no Samantha of *Sex and the City* (Kim Cattrall) without Patsy. Eddy's not sexy, but she is sexual. She is liberated and, despite the fact that she depends on her two ex-husbands' alimony, she is, of course, her own woman, a car crash of emotions that we can all identify with. By all, I mean both men and women. Just because it's about shopping, *Ab Fab* is no girls' club. But by the same token, it is female-empowering. Only Patsy could say 'One snap of my fingers and I could raise hemlines so high the world's your gynaecologist' and get away with it.

Like *Fawlty Towers*, which had so few episodes and yet achieved incredible longevity, there were surprisingly few series of *Ab Fab*. The first was in 1992 and the third in 1996. The last episode of that third series almost felt like the end of an era, but the characters took on worldwide class. The show was almost sold to Spielberg after endless repeats on American cable TV put it on the consciousness there. In the end, Roseanne Barr bought the rights; Saunders no doubt felt it was appropriate that it retained its female-centricity. The satire went beyond dealing with British greyness and political correctness. The themes that French and Saunders had first alighted on – that overindulgence and selfishness are a perfect juxtaposition to the new morality – have become global.

More recently, the series was bought by the French, which encouraged the team to come up with a final series in 2001 – courageously, because everyone feared it would be like yesterday's dinner microwaved. It most certainly was not. The fashions might have changed, but the style could go on forever. Edina still looked the same mishmash of overpowering designers. It's just that the designers were different. Patsy, still smoking, still drinking, was kind of triumphant.

For me, perhaps the moment I felt the full force of its glory was when I was travelling back from Rio on a Varig flight that for some bizarre reason was going via Copenhagen. The in-flight entertainment was nonstop *Ab Fab* dubbed into Portuguese with Danish subtitles. Can I tell you, it was simply beyond.

Alf Garnett
Tony Booth

Alf Garnett, the central character of the seminal television series *Till Death Us Do Part*, is part of the great tradition of comic characters that illustrate the social plight and consequent frustrations of the lower-class man. Although clearly inhabiting a different social stratum to them, the character of Alf Garnett, as realised onscreen by Warren Mitchell, is a memorable achievement of the same order as Charles Pooter in *The Diary of a Nobody* and the lugubrious television persona of Tony Hancock.

Alf Garnett was the personification of a traditional way of life suddenly thrown off balance by the political and social maelstrom of the 1960s. Like generations of working-class people before him, he was a product of his time and place. Alf's life was mapped out from the cradle to the grave in a rigid and for the most part unbending pattern that allowed very little room for manoeuvre or escape. He knew his place in the social and economic order – leaving him, like Pooter, deferential but acutely sensitive to minor humiliations. It is this sensitivity that made his audience feel for him at the same moment they laughed at his pretensions and aggressive pomposity. In the person of Mike, his son-in-law (the part I played in the series), he was confronted by the post-1945 generation who, thanks to a radical Labour government, not only knew they had rights, but were now determined to exercise them. Mike represented a way of thinking and behaving that rejected the restrictions and limitations imposed upon and accepted by previous generations. This sudden loss of deference was frightening and unsettling for Alf (a working-class Tory) just as it was for so many of his generation. Thus Alf not only had to deal with a long-haired interloper married to his adored daughter Rita, he also had to confront the fact that this character rejected all the values and aspirations on which his life was founded – that is: God, Queen and Country. *Till Death Us Do Part* broke new ground in television with its unflinching treatment of all three issues.

God had quite a starring role in the life of Alf Garnett, who had an absolute and unquestioning certainty of His existence and magnificent power. Alf's anxiety in the episode where Mike challenges God to show Himself by striking him dead was genuine. It was unthinkable for someone like Alf to question an absolute given such as the omnipotent and all-seeing Deity. What was interesting about that incident, though, was that, although Mike's desire to torment and frighten Alf was the overriding motive for his behaviour, he himself was not completely convinced there was no risk in the exercise. A sudden bang had both Mike and Alf diving for cover. It was this frailty of both men's egos, and the subsequent jostling for dominance, that was a major factor in the comic tension generated between them. On the one hand there was Alf, whose world was turned upside down by the new order, and on the other there was Mike. The problem with new orders, however, is their very newness, and no one, no matter how confident they may claim to be, can be completely certain where it might take them or just how far one should go.

In Alf's world God was also an indicator of social status, and he was only too aware of the significance of the religion through which one chose to worship. In one particularly inspired episode scriptwriter Johnny Speight had Mike accusing Alf of being Jewish. Alf was driven into a frenzy of something resembling blind panic as he furiously denied the accusation. His reaction to this victimisation stands in stark contrast to his own casual, unthinking and loud-mouthed bigotry – neatly demonstrating that being a victim of racism does not necessarily mean one is therefore not racist oneself. In the days before the Commission for Racial Equality, and public understanding and rejection of the iniquities of racism, Alf's opinions and reactions to 'your darkies' scarcely raised an eyebrow. Racism was endemic throughout the British class structure. Reaction to Alf Garnett was polarised between those who identified with his opinions and those who were appalled by them. Alf Garnett was a relic of the working-class cannon-fodder vital for building an empire. It was necessary to educate people like him to view all foreigners as somehow inferior to the British race – otherwise how would they be prepared to kill or enslave them? In the post-Empire days of the 1960s understanding and rejection of those attitudes was beginning to surface. There is a profound irony in the fact that *Till Death* helped to hasten the dawn of political correctness and thus to ensure that a character like Alf Garnett would no longer be acceptable on our television screens.

Alf's anxiety to keep an authoritarian God pacified came together with his attitude to all foreigners to find expression in his absolute devotion to and respect for the authority of Her Majesty the Queen. He was convinced that, like God, she would look after you, but would also certainly punish any challenges or transgressions. Again, Alf knew the Queen, like God, possessed mystical powers and could see straight into your living room. It was this belief that forced Alf not only to listen to the Queen's speech on Christmas Day, but to stand to attention during the national anthem, despite the jeers and taunts of his family. This was not simply the behaviour of an old reactionary. Alf genuinely believed he was doing the right thing, and it was this characteristic that gave his personality a human edge and prevented him from becoming simply a caricature or a political cipher.

The need not only to belong but to be seen to belong informed Alf's actions and understanding of the world. And just as he was acutely aware that there were people within the class system who looked down on him, he knew and was secure in the fact that, despite his own relatively lowly position, he was able to look down on others. The benchmark of his social status was the ownership of his home, small though it was, and the fact that he had a clean job. Alf wore a waistcoat to work, not overalls. He could not understand the absence of a work ethic in his son-in-law, and it was one of the most frequent sources of friction between them. Much of the tension was generated by Mike's failure, as Alf saw it, to support Rita. Decent men provided for their wives by bringing in

---

Overleaf: *Generation gap: Mike (Tony Booth) and Alf (Warren Mitchell) in* Till Death Us Do Part

a pay packet at the end of each week. Their love for Rita was the one thing the two men had in common. Alf's attitude to his wife Elsie was misogynistic in the extreme – the wife was the one person you definitely had the right to assert authority over, even if, as was the case with Alf, that authority was subverted. Despite his incomprehension at her choice of husband, however, there was no doubting Alf's devotion to his daughter. Again, like his genuine desire to do the right thing as he saw it – respect God and the Queen, provide for his family – Alf's love for his daughter allowed him to be human. When Rita laughed at him we felt his pain and bewilderment and, despite the general awfulness of his personality, felt sympathy. Like all good comic characters Alf offered his audience both recognition and pathos.

In the figure of Alf Garnett we see a man who does not understand that he was, and continued to be, manipulated by the demands of authority and the Establishment. Even when this fact was pointed out to him he could not or would not accept it. How could he? That would have made his whole life a lie. Instead, the great role of Alf Garnett was to be the naïf, the one who held up a mirror to us and reflected back all our fears, failings and frailties – and helped force society to move on.

The Beano *and the* Dandy
Joseph Connolly

A bid of three thousand pounds, anyone? Do I hear four? The fact that these are the sorts of figures that fine copies of the very first issues of either the *Beano* or the *Dandy* can now quite easily command should not really amaze us too much. There is no end to the market for British nostalgia (i.e. oldish and richish types eagerly buying back their childhoods before the onset of mere pre-senility – simple anecdotage – and prior to slipping seamlessly into the big and awful real thing itself). What might come as a surprise, however, in these clever-clever days of prepubescent street wisdom, label obsession and techno-omniscience, is that more than sixty years since their inception, the comics' circulations continue to prosper (the *Beano* alone each week moves about 350,000 copies, and each Christmas both annuals are always bestsellers).

How can this be? How come that these flimsy pre-war products of the famously proud and famously non-union Dundee company D C Thomson can hold up their heads in a world where any diversion that does not plug in, bleep, pass the time of day in Droog-like cyberspeak and encourage virtual and interactive mayhem is viewed by the young with deep-seated suspicion, accompanied by chasmic yawns? The answer, obliquely, is down to the loyalty and persistence of successive generations: which of us hasn't at some point during the rosy past cackled at the mischief of Dennis the Menace or Minnie the Minx, marvelled at the brazen ingenuity of Roger's dodges, or desperately wanted to be Dan (the only adult hero, here, and the sole begetter of designer stubble)? Deep down (and, yes, childishly) no one really wants to let go of any of that, and one therefore does not simply buy the *Beano* and the *Dandy* for one's children, so much as generally bequeath to them for safekeeping both the concept and the history. The built-in bonus, by the way, of such indulgence and altruism is that – supposing one is prepared properly to time the gaps between offspring and then grandchildren (any brief hiatus may be padded out by the odd niece or godchild) – it is perfectly possible never actually to miss a single issue as long as life continues.

The brilliance of D C Thomson's attitude to its comics lies in never too demonstrably rocking the boat (the *Beano*'s current editor is only the third since its founding in 1938), but subtly and constantly evolving in a way that doesn't frighten or alienate the punters, young and old (the *Daily Telegraph* is an old hand at pulling off a similar trick). Some of the gorgeous excesses of the 1950s, though, are – alas – long gone: no more will you see the monocled toff with his black silk topper, spats, spongebag pinstripes and a twinkling diamond tie-stud standing gleeful children slap-up fish suppers at the Hotel de Posh, oblivious to how many ££££ it costs him. If you are lucky you might still spot a Mont Blanc of mash with an embarrassment of bangers cantilevered proudly like the gargoyles on the Chrysler Building – maybe even a perfectly spherical Xmas pud, draped in a mantle of drippy white gooey stuff. Desperate Dan's cow pies, of course – complete with tail and horns (BSE be blowed) – remain the stuff of dreams; he will no longer fashion a pipe, however, from ripped-off guttering and a galvanised dustbin, because smoking, these days, simply cannot be allowed (so even if toffs still abounded, their Zeppelin cigars would be a no-no). Gone too are the catapults (peashooters still linger), as is the predilection for bashings (old *Beanos* of the 1960s had no scruple about Minnie the Minx being set upon by a gang of boys, to be left sprawling with the full array of comic book injuries – not so much disfigurement as a glowing still life with fruit). Nor do any of the many variations on 'Dad' (who is called 'Dad' by his wife, whom he in turn addresses as 'Mum') ritually and with grim-faced relish dole out slipperings in the closing frame. Even Bash Street's 'Teacher' (who is married to 'Mrs Teacher') has hung up his cane. Ah yes, maybe – but not his mortarboard. Now tell me: how common in Britain (let alone Dundee) is a co-educational school comprising just eight pupils and staffed by masters in subfusc gowns and mortarboards? One of the 'Kids' even wears a school cap – and all of them (save Toots, the token girl) are in shorts (as, still, is the great Dennis the Menace himself).

And what do today's *real* kids think? Well, they love it, apparently – instinctively knowing (as we did) that comics have just to be realistic *enough*: no more is required. Few children, for instance, have ever set eyes upon a pile of seeming compost liberally dotted with junk and surmounted by a sign reading 'Town Dump'; but readers of the *Beano* and the *Dandy* know that in their land such a dump will not just exist, but can always be relied upon to yield up a brass bed (on castors and with knobs) and a couple of old upholstery springs (which, when attached to one's lace-ups, will enable one to vault with grace and ease over orchard walls and snaffle apples by mouth before descending crashingly into Dad's boss' cucumber frame); there, too, will be at least one pram (wheels for 'cartie'-making – in Beanoland wooden soapboxes persist) and, by way of garnish, several perfectly preserved skeletons of fish.

There have, of course, been other casualties along the way – most notably, class warfare. The mighty Lord Snooty – he of the top hat and Eton collar – hung on at Bunkerton Castle until the 1990s, when he was quietly retired (though given the state, these days, of the Upper House, where can the poor boy go?); and with him vanished the enemy oiks, the Gasworks Gang.

The innovations over the years have been various, but always pleasingly gradual. Dennis' dog Gnasher (an extremely rare Abyssinian wire-haired tripe hound) is now established as a star in his own right, as is Minnie Mark II: Ivy the Terrible. Cuddles and Dimples are big at the *Dandy* these days – practically babies, but what they lack in years they more than make up for in villainy and destruction. (Their 'Mum', incidentally, is unique in the canon by virtue of being a pretty young blonde in possession of extremely large and globular breasts – all other 'Mums' looking like nothing so much as 'Dads' with wigs on.)

For children of all ages: the Dandy *'Summer Special' of 1965*

For decades, D C Thomson resisted product endorsement of any kind; nor did the comics carry adverts. All that's changed – and every one of our deathless chums may now be seen on video, cable TV and at Beanoland in the Chessington World of Adventures. And as for the fan clubs…! The Dennis the Menace Fan Club long ago enrolled its millionth member and, very tellingly, the more recent *Beano* Fan Club offers its inaugural goodie package and T-shirt in both children's and adult versions. The free gifts still often sellotaped to the front continue to be resolutely non-PC – chewy bars, tooth-crunching lollies and toys that smack of evil, such as the Menacecopter. It's great to be young. Or old. In *Beano* and *Dandy* country, it doesn't really very much matter. We *know* we're now 'Mums' and 'Dads' and 'Teachers' – of course we do; it's just that it's still not, somehow, remotely how we feel.

Beyond the Fringe
Ned Sherrin

It is easier to name John Bassett as the 'Father of Satire' than to define the art and apply the label to *Beyond the Fringe*. Why Bassett? Who Bassett? He earned his jocular title by introducing Jonathan Miller and Peter Cook from Cambridge to Alan Bennett and Dudley Moore from Oxford.

In 1954 Miller appeared in *Out of the Blue*, a Footlights revue which also involved Leslie Bricusse, Frederic Raphael and Patrick Marber's father Brian, who did funny things with an anglepoise lamp. Although Bricusse went on to star with the veteran Beatrice Lillie in her last old-style West End revue, it was Miller's monologues which wowed Harold Hobson when *Out of the Blue* transferred to the Phoenix Theatre: 'A mimic the like of whom has never been seen in the Charing Cross Road… He makes his subjects and unwilling collaborators flow together in a vast, incredible harmony of nature in his superbly funny philosophic fantasy.' He was also a doctor.

Two years later some of Peter Cook's Footlights sketches were promoted to a traditional West End revue, *Pieces of Eight*. The most famous skit featured Kenneth Williams clutching a cardboard box and wheezing, 'I've got a viper in this box'. Funny though Williams was, he was not as persuasive in the role as had been its creator at Cambridge. At the age of twenty-two, Cook came into a kingdom of cash, fashionable celebrity and apparently effortless comedy. As John Bird remarked, 'He was wired up to be funny'.

Back in 1957 Alan Bennett started to make a name for himself in Exeter College, Oxford, 'imitating sermons' and airing them in JCR smokers and college cabarets. In 1959 Bennett, now a junior history lecturer attached to Magdalen, appeared with an Oxford revue team in an Edinburgh Fringe show, *Better Never*. He stole the notices, especially in the *Observer* and the *Daily Herald*.

Three down and one to go. Dudley Moore went up to Magdalen on an organ scholarship in 1954, diversifying into clowning in cabaret and playing traditional jazz at the Union with the Father of Satire's band The Bassett Hounds. The virtuoso improvisational piano player was doubly cherished as someone who could also make a fool of himself. He became an essential part of the Father's strategy. He would supply the witty musical interludes which in the old revues had been provided by girl singers and tight-trousered, bolero-jacketed dancing boys. Rumour has it that at one time Cook fantasised about a very young, scantily clad Julie Christie making periodical crossings of the stage as a running gag. She never materialised. The magic of Moore's spots was that he did not lower the laughter quotient; he maintained it in a radically contrasting way.

Satire can easily be confused with 'send-up', and a way of illustrating why *Beyond the Fringe* doesn't quite suit the label that has become attached to it is to quote Gilbert Highet's magisterial definition: 'Satire deals with actual cases, mentions real people by name… talks of this city and this fresh deposit of corruption whose stench is still in the satirist's curling nostrils.' This was not the ambition of the quartet which the Father convened in a greasy spoon, perhaps on, perhaps off, the Euston Road, in 1960. Bassett had half-abandoned his Hounds to become assistant to Robert Ponsonby, the Director of the Edinburgh Festival. Ponsonby had already made an obeisance to comedy by booking, in previous years, Anna Russell and Flanders and Swann; but the Fringe was running away with his Festival so he commissioned his assistant – grandson of a Gaiety Girl – to find a challenger created on his fiefdom. The quartet remember their tryst variously as 'on Goodge Street', 'in Swiss Cottage' and 'in Warren Street'. One day a playwright will attempt to recreate the egos, emotions, jokes, insecurities, flamboyancies which characterised the meal. No one remembers the menu.

After lunch Bassett took them to meet Ponsonby in his office in St James's. He was wooed and won by their interplay – born of a two-hour intimacy – and promised them *carte blanche* and £100 each. Cook's agent got him another tenner – presumably swallowed up in commission – on account of his professional revue record.

They had their own ideas of what they wanted to be funny about – hence the great solo comic arias. Cook contributed the backbone of most of the group sketches. The revolution was not so much the exposing of each 'fresh deposit of corruption' as the banishment of the anodyne 'tired business man' elements of earlier intimate revues, a new reliance on informed and funny attacks on fresh targets and a consistent challenge to received attitudes and ideas.

Miller made the point: 'I honestly don't think we tried to "do" anything in *Beyond the Fringe* at all.' Cook agreed: 'We don't expect to be specifically didactic.' An observant outsider, John Wells, summed up the attitude: 'They were fooling about on stage in exactly the same way they fooled about off it.' Alan Bennett concurred: 'It has always seemed to me that what was subsequently labelled "satire" was simply this kind of private humour going public.' The nearest he got to a 'sense of purpose' is a sketch of which he guiltily remembers, 'I have a dreadful feeling that I may have thought I was doing some good'.

Away with the chorus girls and boys went the glittering décor and colourful costumes of West End revue. The focus was exclusively on the grey-pullovered performers and their material. A large proportion – sermons, wartime heroes, Shakespeare, journalese and lieder – was parody.

The first sketch in the original running order to deal with 'actual cases, mention people by name' was Peter Cook's impression of Harold Macmillan: 'I went first to Germany and there I spoke to the German Foreign Minister, Herr… [uncertain pause]… Herr and there, and we exchanged many frank words in our various languages, so precious little came of that…'

There was Bennett's famous sermon, by now, he says, 'on automatic pilot, I'd done so many of them'. There was an attempt at an anti-war sketch – 'Whose finger on what button?' – and an End of the World item.

Overleaf: *Jonathan Miller, Alan Bennett, Dudley Moore and Peter Cook in 1964*

After a technically rough first Edinburgh night there was a scatter of notices. *The Times* felt that 'each performer is coolly confident of his own power to amuse and also that the comedy is ruled by a nice sense of proportion'. To Irving Wardle in the *Observer* the script was 'average-level undergraduate revue'. Harold Hobson in the *Sunday Times* found 'touches of irrational genius'. It was Peter Lewis, then the second string critic of the *Daily Mail*, who chanced upon the late-night show and sensed revolution: 'I'd been to those Hermione Gingold revues… I'd quite enjoyed them, but suddenly this was about the real world and one was absolutely astonished.' He wrote prophetically, 'If the show comes to London I doubt if revue will ever be the same again'.

The nearest the cast got to a declaration of intent was the answer to a question put by a student reporter, Michael Billington, who remembers: 'I asked "What are you really attacking? What's your gripe?"… It was "the complacency of Macmillan's England" that they really wanted to get at.'

Beyond the Fringe became the hit of the 1960 Festival, fought over by West End impresarios. Cook's agent Donald Langdon warded them off, having done a deal with a novice producer, William Donaldson. Donaldson made a partnership with Donald Albery, hoping to gain access to a theatre. Albery nearly rocked the boat. After one run-through he announced that 'the fair-haired one [Alan Bennett] will have to go'. According to legend, the cast ran through the show for him twice in the bar of one of his theatres. The first time they performed 'Act One' – including the Cook–Moore sketch about a one-legged man auditioning for the role of Tarzan. By the second occasion, when they revealed 'Act Two', the running order had been changed and the same sketch appeared again. As Albery lacked a leg this did little to endear the team to him. Cut from the original West End programme, it later became a notorious classic.

The show doubled in length when a pre-West End tour opened in Cambridge, and the word 'satire', first whispered in Edinburgh by Peter Lewis, was heard again. Brighton was shocked, particularly by 'The Aftermyth of War', which mocked heroic war films like *The Dam Busters* and *Reach for the Sky*. In London it was welcomed with whoops of joy, particularly by Bernard Levin, who spotted genuine satirical targets in the Prime Minister, Dr Verwoerd of South Africa, Kenya's Mboya, the H-Bomb, the General Secretary of the TGWU, capital punishment, patriotism, Shakespeare, the clergy and antisemitism. However, Michael Frayn, although regarding the London opening of *Beyond the Fringe* as the beginning of the Sixties 'satire boom', emphasised that the greater part of the show was not satirical at all. But there is no doubt that it proclaimed an entirely new attitude. It 'made people laugh at the unthinking attitudes of respect which up to then they themselves had shared'. Or, as Edward Heath was later to say of the impact of *That Was the Week That Was* on television, a direct descendant, it brought about 'the death of deference'.

Beyond the Fringe conquered London and New York. It killed off the old revue form; it was very funny; and it coloured the decades of informed comedy that lay ahead.

The 'Father of Satire' has a lot to answer for.

Blackadder
Sarah Gristwood

It's a truism that fact is often stranger than fiction – especially when you're dealing with history. In Elizabethan days the elderly Earl of Oxford, bending over to bow deeply to his queen, broke wind so loudly the sound was heard even through the padded breeches of the sixteenth century. Mortified, he retired to his country estates, returning only after seven years, by which time he might reasonably have assumed that no one at court would remember the story. He was greeted by a mischievous queen: 'My lord, I had forgot the fart,' she said.

Fact, not fiction. Not even an incident from the second series of *Blackadder* – the one with Lord Percy (Tim McInnerny) and Atkinson's captious courtier Edmund battling with Melchett (Stephen Fry) for the favour of Miranda Richardson as Queenie.

There is a reason why the second *Blackadder* was the first that really worked. It is, in part at least, because we all claim to know a bit about that period of history. We remember a few of the famous stories, like the Armada speech and Raleigh's cloak. Fiction is strongest when it is tied to familiar fact. It's a trick *Blackadder II* pulls off repeatedly.

So much about the series that seems a spoof has its roots in reality. The outrageous flattery demanded by Queenie? There is a letter written by Mary Queen of Scots in which she said Elizabeth I demanded compliments so extravagant that courtiers had to turn their smirking faces away. Queenie's complaint that 'Everyone seems to get married, except me'? The real Elizabeth thought nothing of committing to the Tower courtiers who had wed without her authority. I wrote a book about Elizabeth's cousin Arbella Stuart, who in 1603 was accused of plotting for the throne. She said, in her own defence, that she never really meant all those treasonable approaches. She just wanted to lure the other plotters into showing their hand so she could tell Elizabeth and give the Queen a good laugh at the end of the day… I wanted to quote Baldrick (Tony Robinson) there. Surely even he never had a more (or less) 'cunning plan' than Arbella's crazy fantasy. But it was supposed to be a serious book, and no one would let me.

The first *Blackadder* series, *The Black Adder*, was set in medieval times – something most of us know only from the films of Errol Flynn, and *Robin Hood* or *Ivanhoe* on teatime TV. Something, in other words, that is virtually a spoof already. The great strength of the second *Blackadder* was to put a well-placed poignard up that kind of fake historicity. 'Don't say "beshrew me", Percy,' chides Edmund waspishly. 'Only stupid actors say "beshrew me".' In series II, Edmund Blackadder became the man we laughed with, not the man we laughed at. Like Sid James in a *Carry On* film, or Frankie Howerd in *Up Pompeii!*.

Overleaf: *1917 and all that: the* Blackadder Goes Forth *team*

It's no coincidence that Howerd was a servant cleverer than his master – the role Blackadder would take in the third (Regency) series. From Shakespeare's Fools to Wodehouse's Jeeves, it's an honourable part in British comedy. And *Blackadder* fits into our comic tradition very neatly. We have long laughed at our own past. Before there was *Blackadder* there was *Monty Python* (remember *Monty Python and the Holy Grail, Monty Python's The Life of Brian?*) and *Dad's Army* and *Carry on Henry*.

Long before the screen hits, there was *1066 and All That*, the classic comedy book from 1930: 'A Memorable History of England, comprising all the parts you can remember, including 103 Good Things, 5 Bad Kings and 2 Genuine Dates.' Written by W C Sellar and R J Yeatman, it began life as a series in *Punch* and has been rediscovered by every subsequent generation. 'Elizabeth realised that Mary Queen of Hearts was too romantic not to be executed', wrote Sellar and Yeatman; an apparent piece of nonsense that makes more sense the more you know your history. 'Elizabeth, the Virgin train, had been waiting for ages and ages on the sidelines', wrote Richard Curtis *et al* in *Blackadder: The Whole Damn Dynasty*, the book they did for Comic Relief in 1998. It's the same 'so sharp you cut yourself' humour, though the *Blackadder* team (in the book, at least) scatter their shot a little more widely.

Even before *1066 and All That*, there was Jane Austen's *History of England*, written when she was fifteen for the benefit of her family. 'The Events of this Monarch's reign… are too numerous for my pen, and indeed the recital of any Events (except what I make myself) is uninteresting to me' – there's Charles I pegged by an author who didn't take long to get into her stride. Perhaps Curtis and co should have taken note, because *Blackadder* had a long slow start. We nearly didn't get *Blackadder II*, or the equally popular series III.

The idea was born in 1982 when Rowan Atkinson and Richard Curtis – college friends, and then collaborators on *Not the Nine o'Clock News* – decided to write a sitcom and (to evade, they said, unflattering comparisons with *Fawlty Towers*) to set it back in history. With the help of producer John Lloyd, another *Not…* veteran, they recorded a pilot and then the first half-dozen stories, in which the evil Prince Edmund, aka the Black Adder, attempted to take over the fifteenth-century monarchy. It had a moderate – but only moderate – success. And it cost a lot of money, since it was filmed lavishly in real locations like every other period drama. The combination is never a happy one, and *The Black Adder* was cancelled. End (nearly) of story.

Enter Ben Elton, the motormouth in the spangly suit, and thanks to *The Young Ones* already a hero of the newly popular 'alternative' comedy. He took Atkinson's place as co-author with Curtis: they'd confer, after writing scenes separately. Exit those locations – but the series worked better in front of a studio audience anyway. Enter Stephen Fry and Hugh Laurie, the latter only an occasional visitor in this series, as was Rik Mayall. What with Atkinson and Curtis (who had come out of Oxford in the mid-Seventies), Fry and Laurie (from the Cambridge Footlights a few years later), and now the *Young Ones* duo, Elton and Mayall, *Blackadder* was successfully drawing together many different strands of comedy.

And it didn't hurt that, while *The Black Adder* had tried to overthrow a purely invented monarch, *Blackadder II* took its basis from real history. It was finally aired in January 1986, two and a half years after the last series went away.

The rest, of course, really is history. How McInnerny decided he didn't want to be typecast as another idiot aristo, and was replaced by Laurie for series III. The *Cavalier Years* special for the '88 Red Nose Day, followed by *A Christmas Carol*, with Robbie Coltrane featuring largely. There were always rumours about where the next one would be set. The 1890s? Hippie Woodstock? The team decided on the more controversial 1917 for *Blackadder Goes Forth*, only on condition that they would be able, for the final episode 'Goodbyeee', to do whatever they felt was necessary. It worked: the scene where Blackadder, Baldrick, the objectionable Captain Darling (McInnerny) and Laurie's lieutenant go over the top still features in lists of the most memorable moments on TV. The series had to push the barriers to stay faithful to itself. But the point is that that's what really happened in the trenches. People did die, vainly, tragically.

Perhaps, after all, laughter is the best way to approach some aspects of the past. Beaumarchais wrote: 'I laugh, for fear of being compelled to weep.' It is the classic theory of comedy. You know how an Impressionist painting is meaningless close up, but begins to make sense as you step away? In much the same fashion, comic license gives a necessary distance to the horror of history. Take *Blackadder II* again. How else should you approach a world in which a man might be hung, cut down while still alive, castrated and disembowelled? You were still conscious (unless your relatives paid the hangman to swing on your legs) when they held your testicles up in front of you. By comparison, a baby-eating Bishop of Bath and Wells (Ronald Lacey, in 'Money') looks positively amiable. 'Cold', said Blackadder's aunt Lady Whiteadder (Miriam Margolyes, in 'Beer') 'is God's way of telling us to burn more Catholics.' The reality is almost more chilling: Robert Cecil, the great minister who saw James I succeed Queen Elizabeth, 'confessed' in a letter to a friend that he hated to see Catholics die in their hordes. He knew he was being a big girl's blouse about it. Sorry.

No wonder *Blackadder* is still popular a decade on. No wonder they chose Blackadder and his gang to guide visitors through the centuries in the time-travel film shown in the Millennium Dome. In *Blackadder Back and Forth*, Edmund and Baldrick travel from Roman Britain to a future space war via Sherwood Forest and the Battle of Waterloo. The audience goes too – and returns in safety. Because you know what? The past really was another country. They did do things differently there. And without a return ticket, and the tour rep's phone number in your backpack, it was not one you'd visit too readily.

The Carry On *films*
Rowan Pelling

Carry On films are the Brighton Pier of British comedy; they are the postcards of Donald McGill made flesh and plonked down on a rickety set for two bob a week with a total production schedule of six weeks max. They are to the Hollywood comedy caper what fish and chips are to the Ritz. *Carry On* films appeal to the sort of people who like schoolboy humour, lewd innuendo, sexual stereotyping, bad puns and leering men who say 'Phwoooar!' a lot – in other words, pretty much everyone at one time or another.

British comedy rarely aims for sophistication and succeeds best when it is silly and surreal, like *Monty Python* or Eddie Izzard, or silly and smutty, like Benny Hill and Kenny Everett. As the diverting French film *Ridicule* puts it, while our Gallic cousins have wit, 'the English have something called humour'. And it's true that the broad sweep of British comedy is far better represented by Sid James and Terry Scott than by Noël Coward or Oscar Wilde (who was Irish-born in any case).

The silly/smutty vein of British humour has a long and noble tradition, with striking examples to be found throughout the comedic canon, from mummers' plays and Chaucer's *Canterbury Tales* to Restoration comedy and Victorian music hall. But all these are as minnows when set against the sperm whale of the genre: the thirty-one *Carry On* films, spanning five decades of the last century. The first, *Carry on Sergeant* (1958), was released at the tail-end of the innocent Fifties, when its audience could unselfconsciously enjoy its cheap and cheerful blend of poor production values, great character acting and bawdy humour. The last, *Carry on Columbus* (1992), was a brave but misguided attempt to revive the series in the knowing Nineties, when no audience could safely enjoy tits-'n'-arse jokes, caught as they were between the then rampant political correctness movement and the knowledge that, in just a few clicks of a keyboard, anyone could download eye-boggling pornographic filth from the internet. *Carry On* humour depended on toying gently with society's taboos and incorporating suggestions of 'naughty' words, body parts and sexual acts into their screenplays in a seemingly innocuous manner. A classic gag features Kenneth Williams, as Dr Soper in *Carry on Camping*, saying to Barbara Windsor, 'No, Barbara, tent up first, bunk up later!' But bottoms, breasts and bunk-up jokes ceased to be funny as soon as they were spread over the cover of every lads' mag in the country.

Nowadays the charm of watching *Carry On* films resides partly in nostalgia for a time when women with big breasts were funny, rather than porn stars or millionairess bra models, and wink, wink! nudge, nudge! innuendo was the dizzying height of risqué humour. Only in a *Carry On* movie could a Mrs Moore and a Dr Nookey club together to open 'The Moore-Nookey Clinic' – and you can only raise a laugh from such a laboured gag when comic actors of the calibre of Joan Sims and Jim Dale represent the dubious enterprise.

The stellar quality of the casts, of course, remains the other great reason for watching *Carry On* films. Kenneth Williams, Hattie Jacques, Charles Hawtrey and Bernard Bresslaw are all titans of the post-war, penny-dreadful, domestic comedy scene, while Sid James and Barbara Windsor are the genre's own Bogart and Bacall. And all these actors' names were, and remain, as treasured by British audiences as any Olivier or Redgrave. They became the indelible embodiment of *verboten* stereotypes – battleaxe, pansy, dolly-bird, cockney shyster, moron, etc – that are affectionately retained by the collective memory, even if, in our new, enlightened millennium, nobody dare speak their names. And beyond the recognised stalwarts of the *Carry On* tradition many other celebrated British comedians, such as Frankie Howerd, Leslie Phillips and Terry Scott, graced individual films. You only fully appreciate the acting talent of these comic greats when you set their performances against the dismal showing of their modern-day contemporaries in *Carry on Columbus*: Rik Mayall, Alexei Sayle, Tony Slattery *et al* just didn't have the training, timing or conviction to pull off *Carry On*'s unique blend of wholesome smut. These children of the postmodern world, with its curse of omnipresent irony, are far too knowing to deliver cheeky *double entendres* with the necessary (seeming) innocence.

Continuity was the great strength of the *Carry On* tradition. Gerald Thomas directed every single film and Peter Rogers produced all but *Columbus*. Most of the screenplays were written by Talbot Rothwell or Norman Hudis, and the best-loved *Carry Ons* (for most devotees the first eighteen, up to *Carry on Again Doctor*, 1969) employed the same cast, the same characters and the same situations, with notional changes of scenery, period and plot. No wonder these films went down a storm in Britain, where most of the population fear change and the past is always viewed more kindly than future innovations. *Carry On* appeals to this naturally regressive heart of Middle England, with its love of matron, nursery food and infantile humour. Many adults, myself included, viewed their first *Carry Ons* as children, when the films were regularly paraded over the terrestrial TV channels, and draw on them now for the same comfort factor as boiled eggs and Marmite soldiers. We ask for no more wit and wisdom from them than we did when we were seven. We are happy with characters called Gladstone Screwer and Lady Bettina of Bristol. We are delighted when Charlie Muggins (Hawtrey) says, after his tent's blown away by the MOD, in *Carry on Camping*, 'I knew I shouldn't have eaten those radishes'.

Before I carry fond deprecation too far, it is important to acknowledge that the best of the *Carry On* films take the ridiculous to near sublime heights. Who, having watched it, can forget the scene in *Carry on up the Khyber* where Sir Sydney Ruff-Diamond (James) and assorted officers calmly eat their soup and make polite dinner-party chit-chat as shells bombard the Governor's residence? For a bulls-eye spoof of the British 'stiff upper lip' it has never been bettered. Meanwhile, the keep-fit session where Barbara Windsor's bra pings off her nubile form in *Carry on Camping* remains an iconic moment for wistful males everywhere. And I think most film buffs will agree with me that Burton and Taylor's

Overleaf: *Sid James and Hattie Jacques as Matron in* Carry on Doctor *(1967)*

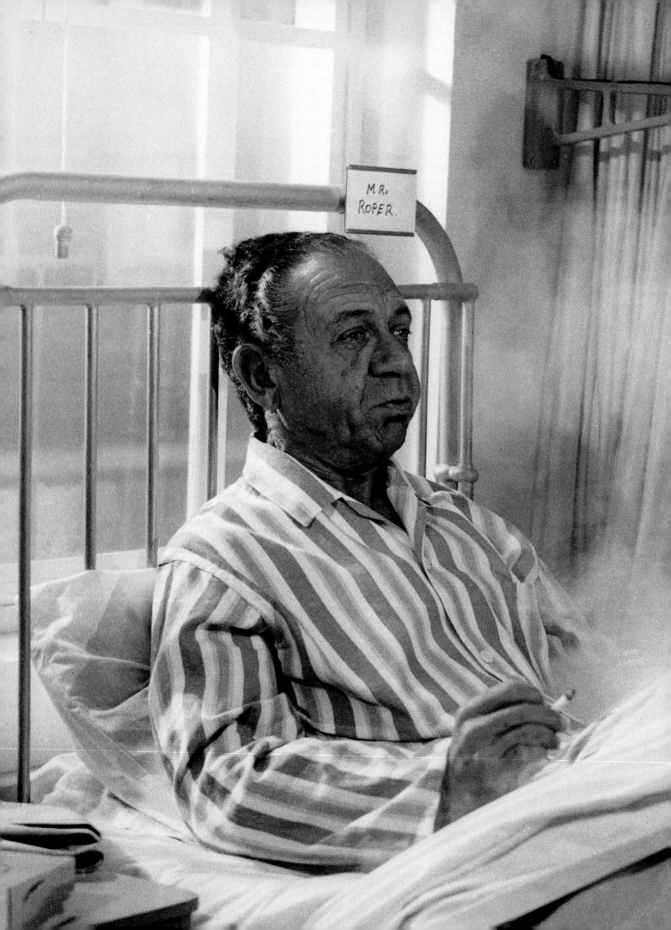

Cleopatra is not a patch on *Carry on Cleo* (both films were released in 1964, and the *Carry On* version cannibalised the big-budget epic's sets and props). Indeed, its most celebrated line – 'Infamy! Infamy! They've all got it in for me!' – delivered with suitable hysteria by Kenneth Williams, was recently voted the ninth most memorable one-liner in cinema history. OK, so Talbot Rothwell stole the gag, with their permission, from Frank Muir and Denis Norden, but it was Williams who made it immortal.

Moments of genius such as this have ensured that the appeal of the *Carry On* genre is not totally parochial. The encyclopaedic fan-site for the films (carryonline.com) is accessed by connoisseurs from more than seventy countries (one regular even logs in from a Pentagon computer), and the films continue their inexorable march from silver screen to small screen to video and now to DVD. Peter Rogers once claimed that his aim was 'to make commercially successful comedies, not great films…' But, as the *Carry On* films' longevity in the public's affection propels them steadily towards the accolade 'classic', it would appear that, despite his best intentions, Rogers is in danger of succeeding on both counts. Accidental triumph, after all, is very much in the finest *Carry On*, and the finest British, tradition.

Charlie Chaplin
Nigel Andrews

For most of the first half of the twentieth century Charlie Chaplin was the most famous person on Earth. His screen appearance was a logo imprinted on every filmgoer's retina, and back then almost everyone *was* a filmgoer. The postage-stamp moustache, the mop of wavy-curly hair, the baggy trousers mismatched with the too-tight jacket, the bendy cane.

He put together this persona and named it as early as 1915 in *The Tramp*. In 1950, still world-famous, it was being imitated – with no fear of non-recognition – by Gloria Swanson in *Sunset Boulevard*. You can watch that film without even noticing Buster Keaton, Chaplin's once-great rival, guesting in a veteran's cameo. But as soon as Swanson's character, to entertain her friends, dons the tramp's gear and does the walk she 'is' Chaplin and everyone, on and off screen, gets it.

Like much greatness, Chaplin's was both terrible and wonderful. The mixture of sentimentality and cruelty in his Little Man character could be slightly frightening. He seduces, then savages. He woos the unwary with winsome oeillades and fluttering lashes; the next moment he brutally boots the target of his disapprobation, who could be any figure of harmless authority from a street cop to a teacher to a barkeeper.

In later films Chaplin's capricious self-ingratiation – the simper combined with the self-righteousness – gets worse. We dislike being lectured by him at the end of *The Great Dictator*, though we applaud the visionary onslaught on Hitler that precedes it. In *Limelight* and *A King in New York* the Chaplin hero seems a mirthless philosopher-clown panhandling for our compassion. By the time he directed Brando and Loren in *The Countess from Hong Kong*, his last, nearly disastrous feature, he was a legend curdling into a liability.

But all myths have their dark or dismaying sides. Chaplin's brilliant side was the uniqueness of his achievement in making universal and iconically resonant an image that started out as barely more than a doodle. For filmgoers the onscreen Charlie was an animated Rorschach test: an inky but distinctive blur capering from movie to movie, allowing each new audience and each new era to see in him their own comical Everyman.

As a hobo-hero looking for mischief in the late 19-teens and early -20s he humiliated the bosses and bullies of an America riven by social inequality. Prohibition brought out the tipsy rebel in him. The Depression made him more comically manic. The war gave him Hitler. The one common thread was his sly fury against the injustices meted out by our 'betters' in the name of national power, civil order or some Pyrrhic blueprint for social and economic prosperity. *The Gold Rush, City Lights* and *Modern Times* all stand as bizarre, inspired outcries against urban dehumanisation and unfeeling technological advance. He lampooned progress when futurism was becoming a fad in art as well as in

Overleaf: *A small cog in a big machine: Chaplin's iconic tramp in* Modern Times

science, thought, philosophy. For Chaplin, Utopia was just a working model for Dystopia, flimsily disguised.

He called himself an anarchist, but really he was a Luddite socialist, if he was political at all. He didn't want change, and that included cinema itself. Nine years after the coming of sound Chaplin was *still* making silent movies (the dialogue-free *Modern Times*). Like his comedy contemporaries Laurel and Hardy, he wanted to eternalise some perfect bygone world in which the have-nots were forever twitting the haves, in which every good man was a sidewalk tramp with dreams above his station.

There are two great coincidences in Chaplin's life. One arranged for him to be born within four days of Adolf Hitler, a virtual twin birth that has spawned a hundred commentaries on the arcane, sinister, portentous symbiosis of these two lives that influenced the course of twentieth-century existence. Semiologists have taken the chance to run riot. Did Hitler model his moustache on Chaplin's, customising his tyrant's upper lip for demotic lovability? Did each man see in the other a mirror-image of demagogic charisma? Did each grow giddy, and finally unstable, on an excess of audience approval?

The other, more subtly prophetic coincidence is that Chaplin came to America on the very same boat as his then equally unknown compatriot Stan Laurel. Both were young troupers with Britain's Fred Karno Company. Chaplin's clown persona could be seen, in long-range hindsight, as some mischievous, anticipatory conflation of Stan and Ollie. The pixilated helplessness of the one is combined with the bullying fastidiousness of the other: which explains why Chaplin can often seem two characters in one, wrestling like cartoon cats in a sack.

His split-personality comic identity may also explain why he couldn't resolve and redefine his screen image once time and changing fashion had obliged him to hang up the tramp costume. Who *is* Chaplin in the later feature films? The only focused comic character he creates is the title wife-murderer in *Monsieur Verdoux*, a Bluebeard comedy as clever and surreal as it is cautionary and a touch scary – as if a little boy lost has grown up to wreak vengeance on the grown-up world that once neglected him.

Chaplin, whose father abandoned the family when the boy was one and whose mother ended up in a mental asylum, could be viewed as a lifelong orphan. He certainly played up to that image: the impish outcast; the vocational misfit; the vigilante loner bent on ridiculing those with too comfortable a niche in the social family. The hints are there for real in an early school photo dated 1897. Amid rows of faces staring straight towards the camera with obedient smiles, Chaplin alone is looking away, holding his head at a fugitive, darting angle as if savouring some recent misdeed or plotting future mischief.

America finally did finger him for a troublemaker. It was enough that this Limey whom they had welcomed into Lotusland held out against taking US citizenship for forty years. But he also attracted undesirable publicity with his womanising, his paternity writs, the scandalous revelations of his sexual habits that emerged during a long-running divorce case.

Once the anti-communists started pawing the ground in the late 1940s, Chaplin's readiness to run off at the mouth on topics like poverty, egalitarianism and social justice made him a marked man. When he heard, on the boat to England where he was sailing to promote *Limelight*, that he was due to be subpoenaed by the House Un-American Activities Committee he just kept on going. He stayed in Europe, settled in Switzerland and swore never to return to America. He broke his vow only when the Hollywood Academy wooed him back for a lifetime Oscar in 1972.

By then his influence was rightly acknowledged to be planetary. He was a legend who was somehow still alive and available for accolade. Chaplin's comedy had spread everywhere, the only legacy of the cinema's early history that had leaped armed and irrepressible into the post-World War Two era. Would we have *Waiting for Godot* without Chaplin? Those two tramps exchanging jokes and tragicomic funny business as they stand by a studio-prop tree? Would we have had the precision slapstick, solipsistic but subversive, of Jacques Tati? Would we even have had Woody Allen, whose breakthrough comedies – *Take the Money and Run, Bananas* – were *tours de force* of physical gag-making, his set pieces essentially silent-comedy riffs involving a little man who was part holy simpleton, part unholy mischief-maker?

The animosity aimed at Chaplin has often been as significant as the applause. A man is flattered by his foes as much as by his friends. For the Nazis to scoff at him as a 'ballerina' was as honourable an endorsement as for George Bernard Shaw to call him 'the only genius developed in motion pictures'. The Nazis may have been more accurate than GBS. Other geniuses have been, and will be, spawned by cinema. But it takes perception, even if ill-intended, to see that Chaplin's polymorphous comic presence is indeed sexually all-inclusive. He was a barroom brawler, yet he could be as finicky and fine-spun as a *première danseuse*. He played plaintive victim as readily as triumphal victor. He knew that no one likes a winner unless he has paid his dues by spending quality time among the downtrodden.

When the French author Balzac called Natty Bumppo, the serial hero of James Fenimore Cooper's frontier adventure novels, a 'moral hermaphrodite' he could have licensed the phrase for re-use. It serves for other great cultural icons whose mystique is mighty enough to span the gender divide and to scorn the distinction between 'weak' and 'strong', 'tough' and 'sensitive', 'meek' and 'macho'. Charlie Chaplin was every one of these, a jack of all contradictions and master of each.

Dick Clement and Ian La Frenais
Bob McCabe

There's a story that Dick Clement and Ian La Frenais used to tell about the time when they were beginning to write *Porridge*. They had the setting, the characters and even some of the plots. But they didn't know what it was *about*. In the interest of research they went to visit an ex-con who had recently been released from prison. He told them that life on the inside 'is all about small victories. Every day you try to score just one more small victory.' That's when they knew they had it. It translates most succinctly as Fletcher saying, 'Don't let the bastards grind you down'.

This attention to details, this finely observed depiction of how real people move in and out of their daily lives, the way their conversation may appear to be about nothing but have real meaning to them, this constant striving to smile or laugh in all the ordinary and adverse conditions of another day, is what has defined the enduring nature of one of British television's most successful comedy-writing partnerships ever.

Dick Clement was born in Westcliff-on-Sea in 1937 and originally had no intention of turning his hand to writing. He wanted to be an actor and was very active in his school drama department. And, like almost every boy of his generation who ended up in comedy, he was an avid listener to the *Goon Show*. After a year as an exchange student in America, and his National Service stint, he answered an advert for a trainee job as a BBC floor manager and was accepted into the Corporation. Once again he sought out the dramatic society, known as the Ariel Players, and started appearing in, and writing material for, their revues. One night in a pub in London he was introduced to Ian La Frenais.

La Frenais was born in Whitley Bay and grew up in the North-east of England. When he and a group of friends decided to try their luck down south in London at the beginning of the 1960s, he had no idea what he was going to do with his life and ended up working in market research. He was introduced to Clement by a mutual friend and, much like the characters they would soon create, the Likely Lads Bob Ferris and Terry Collier, they spent that evening sitting in the pub, drinking, talking and making each other laugh.

They decided to write together, and among their first pieces was a sketch for the Ariel Players called 'Double Date', about two young lads assessing how their double date had gone earlier that evening. The lads were called Bob and Terry. When Clement landed a spot on the BBC's in-house director's course, he and La Frenais decided to adapt 'Double Date' into a filmed television sketch for his final project. The powers that be were so impressed with the finished piece that they quickly decided to try it as a series.

Now the real work began. Clement and La Frenais, who had only ever penned sketches together, had to sit down and write six full half-hour situation comedy scripts, often working in the evening because La Frenais was unable to give up the day job in market research. Then there was casting to consider. The characters were played by Brian Miller and Laurie Asprey in the short term, but once they had seen James Bolam read as Terry, and Rodney Bewes as Bob, they knew they had found their Likely Lads.

There were many unique things about what turned out to be Clement and La Frenais' first major success. Firstly, it was just about the first British sitcom to deal exclusively with young people, not their parents, their olders and betters. Secondly, it was firmly rooted in the North-east of England. Coming from the area himself, La Frenais was eager to give the show a gritty, realistic edge – more importantly a *working-class* edge. The view of the working class that had appeared in the cinema in the early 1960s, in such films as *Saturday Night, Sunday Morning*, *This Sporting Life* and *The Loneliness of the Long Distance Runner* they wanted to transfer to television, with laughs, of course. But still the often tragic edge that permeates those movies is present in *The Likely Lads*. Bob and Terry have dead-end jobs; they try – generally unsuccessfully – to pick up girls; they always inevitably end up round the table in the pub, not crying into their pints but laughing into them at the absurdities of their small, everyday lives.

When Clement and La Frenais revived the series in the 1970s as *Whatever Happened to the Likely Lads?* these elements were even more prominent. Although we were apparently living in a classless society, the show was firmly all about class, as Bob moved slowly into the middle class, leaving his friend stuck behind, still content with a pie and pint because he can see no option of anything else. This was a sequel about growing up, growing away – and in a curious way about men who love each other, but haven't got the facility to say so. It remains the most bitter-sweet work the two writers ever did, and for many their best.

Not to say these shows weren't funny. *The Likely Lads* was the first sitcom aired on BBC2 and was an instant hit with critics and the new channel's limited audience. When it was repeated on BBC1 months later to huge audiences it established Clement and La Frenais as one of the leading comedy-writing teams in television, praised alongside the likes of Ray Galton and Alan Simpson. *The Likely Lads* ran for three series and afforded Clement and La Frenais the opportunity to branch out into movies, penning a variety of projects ranging from *Hannibal Brooks* to the Richard Burton thriller *Villain*, but despite such later successes as their adaptation of Roddy Doyle's *The Commitments* they never really hit their stride on the big screen. They simply played best in the living room.

In 1973 the team met with Ronnie Barker to discuss writing two one-off half-hour scripts for his new series *Seven of One*. One of these was set in a prison, the other was called 'I'll Fly You for a Quid', with Barker cast as the patriarch of a Welsh family of inveterate gamblers. When the BBC asked Barker which one he wanted to develop as a spin-off sitcom, he opted for the latter. Thankfully, the BBC overruled him and went for the prison one.

The pilot, 'Prisoner and Escort', developed into another of Clement and La Frenais'

Overleaf: *Godber (Richard Beckinsale), Fletcher (Ronnie Barker) and Mr McKay (Fulton McKay) in* Porridge

biggest successes – *Porridge*, a show that truly was about 'small victories', as Barker's Norman Stanley Fletcher spends his five-year jail stretch constantly battling with the authority of the screws around him, while never letting them see that he is fighting at all. As with the best of their series, *Porridge* featured near-perfect casting, strong ensemble playing, eloquently funny scripts and that sense of the characters being real people, whose lives and conversations the audience was just dropping in on. Like *Whatever Happened to the Likely Lads?*, *Porridge* is firmly rooted in the class imbalances of the mid-1970s. It is the oppressed underclasses scoring one against those in charge. Both it and *Whatever Happened to the Likely Lads?* transferred to the big screen, though both shows were far better suited to the thirty-minute form.

By the mid 1970s Clement and La Frenais had moved to Hollywood, although they continued to work for British television on such further sitcoms as *Thick as Thieves* and the less successful *Porridge* sequel *Going Straight*. One of the advantages of living in Hollywood is that they soon became highly paid 'script doctors' – those uncredited beings drafted in to beef up a screenplay. Sean Connery asks for them personally, and they worked behind the scenes for him on such movies as *Never Say Never Again* and *The Rock* (indeed the former movie, Connery's last stab at being Bond, includes a gag lifted directly from the *Porridge* pilot).

In the Thatcherite Britain of the 1980s, Clement and La Frenais – despite their secondment to Hollywood – once again created a series that captured the working-class mood of the time. The unlikely tale of a group of British builders forced to find work in Germany proved the boys could write in a sixty-minute format, blend genuinely moving drama with sharp comedy and produce another critical and audience favourite. They are primarily best as writers of male characters – they understand how men think and talk when they are alone with each other – and *Auf Weidersehen, Pet* highlighted a broader canvas of characters than their previous series. When the show was revived in 2002 many thought these Eighties outcasts would have lost their relevance. Given the fact that this latter-day sequel had the boys building a bridge for a tribe of Native Americans in Arizona, hopes were not high. But once again the writers proved to have their finger bang on the pulse. In many ways this revival was a sort of 'Whatever Happened to Auf Weidersehen, Pet?' – a group of men, bound together by their younger days, now faced with the reality of it all slipping away, trying to get by before it's too late. It was as popular, as poignant and as funny as anything they have ever written.

Dick Clement and Ian La Frenais are a remarkable force in the history of British television comedy. Their output over the past forty years is unequalled, and certainly never bettered. To have created one classic television series would be enough for anyone. To have done it five times is simply amazing.

The Comedy Store
Sandi Toksvig

Despite having no training whatsoever for the job, I have spent nearly a quarter of a century working as a comedian. I did, however, study to be a lawyer so here is

A caveat:
I forget the actual statistic but there are a worrying number of people who think Joan of Arc was Noah's wife. Not that the educated among us can gloat. I bet most people would be hard pushed to tell your basic Richard II from your Richard III or recall the exact reasons why Hitler ever thought that moustache was a good idea. This absence of knowledge doesn't worry me unduly. I'm not sure there is a lot of point to history. It's mostly just stories of men in overcoats bossing about men without overcoats while the women stay at home and do the real work. No one ever learns anything from it: 'The First World War was horrid so let's have another one…'

So I am owning up to being a sceptic about any attempt to report the past accurately or with perspective, and that includes the bits I was there for. My father was a foreign correspondent and I spent my childhood trailing around behind him to big events. I was as close as any human being when Apollo 11 was launched at Cape Kennedy heading for the moon, and I saw Neil Armstrong step out onto the lunar surface on the giant screens inside mission control at Houston, Texas. Could I write the history of the space programme? No. On a slightly smaller scale of significance, I was there on the very first night that the London Comedy Store opened. I was there on the night the tenth anniversary of the Store was celebrated with an all-female bill of comics. For many years I was there every Wednesday and Sunday night. Can I write an accurate history of the place? No. I can just tell you what I remember and what it felt like.

I don't feel bad about this. I have been around long enough to have read books about the past in which I am included. On the whole, the descriptions bear no relation to my recollection whatsoever. I started my career on the comedy stage at Cambridge University in an ancient society for humour called the Footlights. Someone called Robert Hewison has published a history of the club which has little in common with what I think happened in my three years of membership. (He also spells my name wrong, but I've got over it.) There is another author who has written about the Store for years. He could probably publish what he would believe to be an accurate history of the place. My only concern is that he did once review an event I was in before it had happened, which I believe to be a unique understanding of the word 'review'.

Right. That is my caveat. Here is what I recall of

Overleaf: *Jenny Éclair mimics the logo of the Comedy Store during its twentieth anniversary show, 1999*

The Comedy Store:

May 1979 – I had just turned twenty-one, on the same night that Margaret Thatcher came to power. I was finishing my second year at college, and I didn't know it then but I was not well. I had a growth expanding in my system which meant I couldn't eat but had a stomach no pregnant woman would be ashamed of in her final trimester. With the arms and legs of a famine victim and the belly of Michael Winner, I was a curious sight. Soon I would be spending my summer in hospital, but until then I was doing comedy with my university pal, Simon McBurney. Simon had, and still has, the most malleable face I have ever come across. He could just give me a look and make me laugh. He and I had developed a kind of double act in which he said nothing and I spoke a great deal. It probably played to both our strengths. Simon has since grown up to do great things with his theatre company Théâtre de Complicité.

I don't remember how it came about, but Simon got an invitation to appear at a new comedy club which was opening in the West End and he asked me to go and 'do the act'. At the time he was going out with another young thing called Emma Thompson. (I don't know what happened to her, but she was charming.) Simon, Emma and I took the train from Cambridge and headed to the big smoke in the south.

Our education at Cambridge having fitted us for nothing except detailed analysis of syntax, we were innocents abroad. To us, performing in the West End represented glamour. To Don Ward, the man behind the Comedy Store, it represented a small room above a strip club. The Gargoyle Club on, I think, Meard Street was probably not a place people usually went to for laughs. Don had had posters printed with the words 'Comedy Store' in black and red, and had pasted them over the club's normal backlit display boards. Unfortunately, the paper was cheap and the Gargoyle's normal bill of fare could easily be seen bleeding through. Women with astonishing mammaries, and one blonde who seemed to have an unnatural fondness for her dog, leered at the would-be comedians.

Inside the place was dark, with the welcoming smell of disinfectant on beer-washed nylon carpeting. Upstairs the woman behind the bar was cross: 'This is supposed to be a doubles bar. How can anyone see my doubles if I have to wear a shirt?' I had no idea.

The host for the evening was an American man who sold pizzas for a living. He had an act which consisted of reading out bits from his high school year book. Pizza man was explaining to a nun that if she didn't get laughs then he would hit a brass gong and she would have to get off. 'Oh, we can't do that,' declared Simon and I adamantly. 'We have a set piece and we couldn't possibly get off in the middle.' I think the host was so surprised at our gall that he agreed. I don't recall much about the rest of the evening. I don't think many people came. I do know that the nun got the gong and we didn't. Simon and I did our piece, with Emma in the wings providing sound effects with a football rattle. I have no idea if anyone laughed. I doubt it. We must have been a bizarre sight – a silent, spiky-haired gurner and a woman with the physical allure of Mr Potato Head.

It was some years later that I returned. By now the club was doing well and had moved to a basement in Leicester Square. It was a Sunday night and the place was as empty as the old Gargoyle Club, with little improvement in the smell. I had come to watch improvisation at the invitation of an old Cambridge acquaintance, Neil Mullarkey. The foot-high stage was made of black boxes shoved together to form a tiny rectangular performance area. A small group of performers, the fledgling Comedy Store Players, were making up sketches based on audience suggestions. It wasn't easy as there were hardly enough audience members to spell each word. Pretty soon I was up there accepting Serbo-Croat as a suggestion for an amusing foreign language. (Little did I know then that Serbo-Croat would be what people always suggested when asked for an amusing foreign language.) Business was not good. Don paid us all in free beer. One free beer. Then he decided that things really were so bad that the six improvisers would no longer get beer but receive instead a percentage of the nonexistent box office. We got 60 per cent between us. I suspect it was a decision he was to regret. Within six months the place was selling out.

Despite the presence of females like myself, Josie Lawrence, Jo Brand and Jenny Éclair, the Store, like every other comedy club in London, was a boys' domain. Women were few and far between, and certainly not catered for. The dressing room consisted of a small, narrow space with a single sink at the end. Here, the boys freely relieved themselves, as indeed would Josie and I in times of desperation. I moved on to doing some stand-up, and ten years after that first night at the Gargoyle Club I helped host the first ever all-female night of comedy at the Store. It was one of the best evenings of my professional life. All the male comics stood in a row, beer in hand, and watched in silence as we stormed the place. Were women finally taking their place at the forefront of laughter? No. Such a bill has never happened again.

I haven't been to the Store in years. Indeed I don't even know where the new one is. It was a hugely important place in the history of comedy in this country. If you go one night, have a look around. I'm sure somewhere Don will have the framed bill from that very first night. About half way down the list it says 'Simon McBurney and Sandy'. He never got my last name and he spelled my first one wrong. That's a historical record for you. But I was there.

Billy Connolly
James Naughtie

Billy Connolly is one of the few men who can seem at home with a banjo. Whether he is finger-picking or strumming it, this strange instrument, with its neck too big for its body and its funny metallic sound, catches something of his personality. Like his banjo – and despite the fact that it's a long time since he's worn his banana boots or his outsized wellies – he's an incarnate joke. The straggly beard, the falsetto giggle, the look of perpetual surprise – they're the comic apparatus of someone who knows that people can't help being funny if you look at them in the right way.

I first heard that banjo sometime in the Sixties, when he used to play with Gerry Rafferty and they called themselves The Humblebums. The Shetland fiddler Aly Bain was a frequent co-conspirator in their rambling concerts, and there never seemed much difference between what happened on stage and what went on in the bar afterwards. Connolly's contribution to those nights of riotous good nature was often some jangling blues or a song plucked from the fringes of the country music that has always appealed to him. Most of all, there was the patter. He couldn't stop talking, spinning yarns and laughing at the absurdity of so many of the people he knew, and painting a wild picture in vivid technicolour of his own place, Glasgow. It was from these nights on the road, and the thread of these stories, that Connolly the Seventies entertainer sprang, fully formed, as a selfconsciously unruly national treasure.

This transformation from jobbing singer and storyteller to international star was one of the most extraordinary comic happenings of our time. Suddenly, Connolly was on world tours. His records were selling millions, and aged aunties were chuckling with him, even when he was telling shaggy dog stories about the crucifixion or discussing the rights and wrongs of farting in the bath. In 1975 his immortal take-off of the country and western style in 'D.I.V.O.R.C.E.' (and three of his other records) were gold bestsellers, and the next year he was off to Australia and to the United States with Elton John. This was the year when the world outside Glasgow discovered the Big Yin and a particular brand of humour.

His appearance on Michael Parkinson's chat show in the course of that year was a moment of high and memorable farce. It was as if this gangling, hairy banjo-player, who'd starred in something called *The Great Northern Welly Boot Show* and told endless stories in Glasgow dialect, had suddenly thrown his arms and legs up in the air and flipped over the high-jump bar. No one had seen it done before. Overnight, it seemed, everyone was telling the story which had reduced Parky to hysterical tears – the one about the man who said he'd murdered his wife that morning and buried her, then showed off

---

The Big Yin: Billy Connolly in 1988

her backside sticking out of a mound of earth outside his tenement 'because he needed somewhere to park his bike'. Connolly was taking people to places they hadn't visited before, and doing it without the 'alternative' label that would weigh down so many of those who would follow. This was raw and risky humour, but it didn't seem to be a new view of the world, just the world described in a different voice.

Connolly's trick – or, rather, his natural gift – is to draw on traditions that we all understand and know. He isn't a breakaway from the kind of comedy that preceded him, but actually a kind of homage to it. He comes, after all, from Glasgow, where the Empire was the famous music hall graveyard, its gods packed with the most devastating one-line critics in the business – the kind of people who could choose their moment to send down, just as Mike Winters was joined on stage by his brother at the start of their act, the rasping observation: 'Oh no. There's two o' them.' The music hall days were still alive when Connolly was young, and a string of Scottish comedians, many of them spectacularly lugubrious clowns, would pace the stage of the Pavilion or the Empire or the Kings philosophising on the events of the city and its people. Connolly didn't break with that tradition. He celebrated it with a giggle.

The secret, of course, is Glasgow's obsession with itself. The city loves to wallow in its own reputation for a kind of hard-edged sentimentality, where conmen and gangsters and shambling drunks are the great characters of the street and keep up a running commentary on their life and times in a rich and intoxicating patois. Connolly became an interpreter of all this to the world outside, and the reason he succeeded was that it was done with a bubbling affection that stripped his act of any bitterness. The people he spoke about, whether they were being mocked for their middle-class pretensions or for their working-class sensitivities, were people he seemed to like. He has never stopped laughing at his own jokes, and a Connolly monologue always involves long detours from the central story, with regular pauses for those unmistakeable giggles and gasps of delight, no matter how often he has told it before. During the Seventies the act was polished and carefully staged, but it was never artificial.

He leapt across boundaries that had seemed insurmountable, especially on television. From the moment Kenneth Tynan said 'fuck' on air in the Sixties – though Peregrine Worsthorne also claims credit for the first one – it was only a matter of time before a comedian would be able to perform on television as he might do in a pub. Connolly was soon telling stories about all the bodily functions that make him laugh so much, about masturbation and messy sex and religion, and sprinkling the whole performance with words that hadn't been the usual currency of the stage. He survived because of the good nature of it all. When the two Celtic supporters visit Rome and go on a bender, deciding to honour their religion by drinking whatever it is that the Pope drinks and settling on *crème de menthe* by the pint, they find themselves in the gutter desperately ill at the end of the night and one says wearily to the other: 'See, Michael, if that stuff's whit the Pope drinks, nae much wonder they carry him aboot in a fuckin' chair.' And even when he's not talking about *his* people, the people who were welders on Clydeside like him or who drank in the old bars around the Barras market, he is still a soft-hearted critic.

When he was a guest on *Desert Island Discs*, he chose a recording of pipes and drums playing 'The Skye Boat Song', a piece that generations of scrubbed Scottish schoolchildren would sing by the piano, and a song associated more with middle-class drawing rooms than with smoky bars. He has an ambiguous love for it all, like his attraction to the country and western tradition. He can take it apart, but then you feel he wants to put it back together again. When he picks up his banjo he is as likely to play Hank Williams as Leadbelly.

As he approached sixty, he acknowledged all this by buying an estate in Aberdeenshire. As Laird of Candacraig, he can relax on Royal Deeside and introduce his Hollywood buddies to the joys of the annual Lonach Gathering in August – the local Highland games, which start with the traditional March of the Lonach Men, kilted locals who are set up for their day's exertions with large drams of malt whisky served by the Laird. For Connolly, the irreverent scourge of all things twee, and the particular rituals that Scots have come to know as Balmorality, this might be thought an unlikely Shangri-la. Not at all. It's the proof that he's a softie through and through.

The spectacular success of the biography written by his wife Pamela Stephenson revealed how precious to us this character has become. It's a remarkable story of a rough childhood and sexual abuse that he couldn't talk about for nearly forty years, the tale of a character moulded in the shipyards and the street, in drink-fuelled nights on the road with the band and in the heady days of early fame. Being with Connolly is always a party, even since he turned away from the bottle, and wherever he is he'll start something going. Parky has a story of being with him in Sydney on a terrible drinking spree and discovering that he'd leapt out of their taxi to do a Fred Astaire impression in the middle of the late-night traffic, grabbing passers-by to play Ginger Rogers. This sort of thing has happened on several continents and in nearly every town and village in Scotland.

He's always laughing. When he was filming *Mrs Brown*, playing John Brown to the Queen Victoria of Judi Dench, there were huge gaps in the proceedings for laughter and stories. He's even said to enjoy the often hostile reaction to the silly ads he did for the National Lottery wearing a purple beard: many funny men would be touchier and want to forget the whole sorry thing.

Underneath the wellies and the beard and the banana boots, the symbols of his early success, there is a sometimes mournful clown and a life which has had its share of pain. But on the outside, there's fun. Billy Connolly's secret is that he makes people laugh because he never stops laughing himself. And it's very hard indeed not to join in.

Tommy Cooper
Barry Cryer

Icon/Ikon – (1) A representation of Christ or a saint. (2) An image, picture, etc. (3) A symbol resembling or analogous to the thing it represents. (4) A person regarded as a sex symbol or as a symbol of a belief or cultural movement. (5) A pictorial representation of a facility available on a computer.

To say the least, none of the above quite describes Tommy Cooper, with the possible exception of 'A symbol of a belief or cultural movement'. And yet, in my frequent travels among the younger members of the comedy tribe, Tommy is often referred to as an icon – maybe they regard him with something approaching religious fervour.

Like Laurel and Hardy, he seemed to embody the very basics of comedy, boiling it down, distilling it to the very essence. All right, the word I'm groping for is 'funny'.

We didn't use the word 'stand-up' to describe a solo comedian when I started, but I can't think of a neater definition. It implies, for instance, 'stand up and be counted', and that's exactly what we do – naked, exposed, desperate for love or, failing that, laughter.

Paralysis by analysis. Get to the point, aged droll.

As a stand-up, Tommy certainly stood up further than most. I once described him as 'Mount Rushmore on legs'. The face was unmistakeable – but not inimitable. He must have been the most imitated comic ever. And yet no one ever approached the real thing. Incidentally, if you *did* approach him, you were liable to depart somewhat bewildered but always amused.

J B Priestley has a theory that great comedians are extra-terrestrials, visitors from another planet, descended among us to amuse and bemuse. Think of Les Dawson, think of the great Ken Dodd. Have you ever known anyone who looked *quite* like them? Answer on one side of the paper only, please. Les once, or rather frequently, described himself as looking as if he had been hit by a lift, and Doddy is the very embodiment of dragged through a hedge backwards after getting out of bed fully clothed. Tommy? Well, think the Golem, think an Easter Island statue come to life.

After that searing visual diagnosis, I think the least I can do is to return to the bottom line – how funny he was. To me, that is, and to so many others – maybe not to you. Comedy is a subjective thing; people take it very personally. They use emotional words like 'love' to describe a person who makes them laugh and 'hate' and 'can't stand' for someone who doesn't. Comedians themselves use expressions such as 'killing an audience' for going well and 'dying' for the reverse.

But if a comic consensus were to be taken, I hazard a guess that Tom would secure a

'Just like that': Tommy Cooper, the most imitated comic of all time

pretty impressive majority. Eric Morecambe, no slouch he in the comedy stakes, once said to me *re* Tom (by the way, please get accustomed to the sound of names being dropped in this treatise), 'That bugger just has to walk on and they laugh – I have to start working'. Typically self-deprecating, but an acute observation nonetheless.

The height, the feet, the fez, that face. Bewitched, bothered and bewildered – the mood only broken by the throaty laugh. He was a manchild, totally at sea in an adult world, but still a knowing innocent. Shortly after coming on stage, he would look into the wings and say: 'Come off? I've only just come on.'

And of course, the tricks. He was a member of the Inner Magic Circle and I can testify to his skill at card and coin manipulation – 'close up magic' as it's known. His pockets were invariably full of the aforementioned cards, coins and other small props, and he would launch into a routine at the drop of a fez.

Talking of which, it has to be said that if Tom wasn't the focus of attention, he would sulk. He seemed to have no interest in, or knowledge of, current affairs, politics and such. This was reflected in his act: just jokes and tricks, but not a single contemporary reference. This is probably the reason for his timeless appeal – nothing he said or did dated, rather like Morecambe and Wise.

The legend goes that at an audition, due to nerves, he bungled several tricks and realised that his ineptitude was getting laughs. Whether or not this is true, he once said to me that there were many good magicians, but not many funny ones. There had been the Great Valentine in America, a man who would proudly open his jacket to reveal medals he had won for his artistry, and in France the wittily named Mac Ronay, who by a strange coincidence wore a fez, albeit smaller than Tom's. It amused me that Tom always denied any knowledge of Mac. No matter, he (Tom, that is) was still an original in his own right.

After a career spent in theatres, and at the height of his celebrity as one of Britain's best-loved television acts, he transferred his attention to the newly burgeoning world of clubs. This was in the Seventies, and it was not an environment for the faint-hearted. Hot, smoky rooms resounded to the noise of clinking glasses and the constant clang of fruit machines. Not to mention frequent interruptions from drunken hecklers. Tom was appearing at the Golden Garter in Manchester and during the week bumped into a friend who asked if he was coping. Tom replied that he was. 'What about hecklers?' 'That's all right, I bought a book of heckler-stoppers in America.' (Heckler-stoppers are putdown lines to counter any interruptions from the audience.) The word went round about Tom's debut in this dangerous world, and several acts, including Eric and Ernie, decided to go and see him on the Friday night. Eric Morecambe told me that there were some four tables of Tom's peers, eagerly awaiting the great man's entrance. A digression: the opening of Tom's act was unique – the band would play his signature tune 'The Sheikh of Araby' and he wouldn't come on. I repeat: he *wouldn't come on*. After a deathless pause, the audience would hear his voice, muttering that he was locked in his dressing room. This was, of course, Tom behind the curtain, on a microphone. I can vouch for the fact that it was one of the funniest openings of an act I have ever seen. He would then emerge, to rapturous applause.

Back to Friday night at the Golden Garter. Tom had duly come on and plunged into his customary orgy of jokes and chaotically delivered tricks. In the middle of his act a waiter tripped on the carpet and deposited a whole tray of drinks on the floor, right in front of him, with a resounding crash. Eric told me the moment was electric. You could have heard the proverbial pin. Tom looked down. 'That's nice,' he said. To an audience eagerly awaiting some devastating comment, this banal utterance was so in character that it was the funniest thing he could have said, as the resultant laugh testified.

This flair for knowing exactly what suited him was a key element in his success. Many (if not all!) his jokes were singularly lame on paper, but with his delivery he made gold out of dross. His timing was instinctive and he had an endearing indifference to the technical aspects of comedy. One of his favourite jokes was: 'A man walked into a bar and went, Ooooh! It was an iron bar.' (See what I mean about his jokes on paper?) He put the stress on the word 'bar', not 'iron', which, in my boring pedantic way, I considered to be essential. I pointed this out to Tom and he gazed at me, uncomprehendingly. 'Did they laugh?' he said. 'Yes,' I admitted. 'Shut up,' he growled. And then laughed.

What can you say about a man who walked on a stage or cabaret floor and suddenly noticed a pedal bin before him? He gazed at it, nonplussed. Then he walked over to it, spotted the pedal and, after some hesitation, pressed it with his foot. Naturally, the lid flew open. The look of childlike joy on his face was ecstatic. Thenceforward, throughout his act, he would spot the bin and repeat the process, sometimes with his back to it, sometimes sneaking up to surprise it. You had to be there; it was comic genius. ('*Genius* – Person with exceptional ability, especially of a highly original kind.' I rest my case.) In a similar way, he would sometimes have a small gate on the stage, with fencing on either side. This would be discovered, like the pedal bin, and from then on Tom would walk through it, carefully closing it behind him. Funny? Ask any audience who witnessed this bizarre incident and they will tell you.

He died on TV, during the ironically named 'Live from Her Majesty's'. That night, Eric Morecambe said to me on the phone: 'How sad – poor Tom, going in front of the audience.' Six weeks later, Eric died, but he got off the stage first.

Tom defied analysis, but I've tried some. I'll finish now. Just like that.

Dad's Army
Ray Connolly

If we were to ask the top British comedy writers of the past thirty years to nominate their favourite British situation comedy of all time there's little doubt in my mind that the overwhelming choice would be *Dad's Army*. Virtually no one in the business of making people laugh has a single unkind work to say about it, which makes this programme something unique. Rarely do professionals and public so happily agree.

But *Dad's Army* is more than Britain's consistently favourite programme, as evidenced by the endlessly repeated showings on television more than a generation after it was first screened. It is also an affectionate view of how the entire nation sees itself – the *Dad's Army* platoon and their adversaries, the verger and the air raid warden, being a gentle microcosm of British society.

The situation might be the Home Guard in the small, fictional Sussex town of Walmington-on-Sea during World War Two, but the petty rivalries, the little pomposities and the well-meaning incompetence of the corps could, and still can, be seen in any office or organisation in the country. Indeed, the genius of the programme lay in the way the writers of the show, Jimmy Perry and David Croft, took the very essence of Britishness (class, a sense of history and small-town self-importance) and by setting it in the heightened atmosphere of wartime held a mirror up to national attitudes and characteristics which prevail eternally. In short, it makes us laugh at ourselves and our foolish ways.

The great idea was that although this is a series about wartime, it's one where no one ever gets killed. There are no War Office telegrams of loss, no sense of terrible things happening just across the Channel. And when a troupe of Germans do turn up, our heroes quickly find themselves taking orders to buy them fish and chips.

Although it took about eighteen months to become a national favourite, everything about *Dad's Army* worked from the very first programme in 1968. Although much of the camerawork illustrates the tiny budgets of the time, everything else was perfect. For a start there were the comic graphics of the opening titles: the advancing Nazis snaking across the Low Countries, menacing the Channel and being faced there by the pulsing arrows of Union Jacks. Then there was the signature tune. The original idea was to get Vera Lynn to sing something suitably wartime-sounding, but Jimmy Perry, who dreamed up the series, decided to write the theme himself. The result, cleverer than any pastiche but completely encapsulating the mood of the series and the time, has become a national classic. 'Who Do You Think You Are Kidding, Mr Hitler?' sang Bud Flanagan, one half of the old musical hall duo of Flanagan and Allen, to the accompaniment of the Band of the Coldstream Guards. Even before the programme starts we're smiling at the idea of this band of defiant, plucky Little Englanders, men like Mr Brown who goes up to town on the eight twenty-one, but who, back for his Home Guard duty in the evening, is ready with his gun. And for over thirty-five years we've been laughing at the seventy-seven surviving episodes.

For many years now television has been awash with documentaries and dramas about World War Two, but when *Dad's Army* first appeared in 1968 the Home Guard had virtually disappeared from public memory. Recollections of wartime were mixed, and when it was first previewed to trial audiences the responses were disappointing. Luckily the nerves of the BBC held, not least because producer David Croft ignored the unsatisfactory responses.

But why was it so successful? Why did it triumph when so many other shows failed and were forgotten? The reasons are many and varied, but two override all others. The first is character. Every man in the platoon, from Captain Mainwaring to Pike, the 'stupid boy', is instantly recognisable and true. We all know people just like them. Indeed, there is a truth about everything in *Dad's Army* – a genuineness which comes directly from the series having been born out of the creator's own experience.

When Jimmy Perry first conceived *Dad's Army* in 1967, with the unlikeliest provisional title of 'The Fighting Tigers', he was an unsuccessful repertory actor. Already in his early forties, he was working in Joan Littlewood's Theatre Workshop, wondering why, after seventeen years slogging around the country, fame and success had eluded him. His original plan was simply to write a TV series with a part in it for himself – since few other series' producers wanted to take him on – and with that in mind he created the role of Walker, the spiv. Wiser heads would soon convince him that he could hardly act in *and* write the series without antagonising all the other actors, but in trying to make work for himself he not only switched careers, but accidentally created a classic.

The secret of his success was that he wrote about what he knew. As a boy of seventeen in Watford in 1941, he'd joined the Home Guard (like Pike in the series – although Perry insists he never wore a scarf). There, he discovered that his first commanding officer was the manager of a local building society – who would one day be not a million miles from the character of the bank manager Captain Mainwaring. The more Perry remembered of his boyhood wartime experiences, the more he realised their potential. All around him in the Home Guard had been characters just waiting to be fleshed out into comedy. There was even a character who (like Corporal Jones, the butcher) had actually been at the Battle of Omdurman in the Sudan in 1898. (Whether he ever said 'they don't like it up 'em, sir' is not recorded.)

Little by little, Perry and David Croft, who became his co-writer on *Dad's Army* and several other projects, researched the Home Guard through newspaper cuttings libraries. And, character by character, the platoon was built up: to Walker, Pike, Mainwaring and Jones were added Private Godfrey with the weak bladder, who always needed to be excused – too old, in fact, ever to have been in the Home Guard, but a delightfully dotty character; and Frazer, the wild-eyed, doom-laden jeremiah of a Scotsman who runs the local undertakers.

Overleaf: *'Who do you think you are kidding, Mr Hitler?': the* Dad's Army *platoon*

But best of all was the relationship between Arthur Lowe as the pompous, plump, grammar school educated branch bank manager and his second-in-command, John Le Mesurier, the public school, slightly effete Sergeant Wilson, with his gentle orders to the troops: 'Would you mind awfully falling in, please.' For some, the notion that an ex-public schoolboy should be of a lower rank than a grammar school boy in the class-ridden armed forces seemed unlikely, a reversal simply for comic effect. Not so, says Jimmy Perry. Although class may have defined one's status in the real fighting forces of the Army, Royal Navy and Royal Air Force, in the Home Guard it counted for very little. So, comic though the relationship is, it too was based on truth.

Captain Mainwaring would always be the butt of the show, but the jokes against him were never cruel. Week in, week out, he was made to look a fool as he tried to rally his platoon, but it was always clear that there was a huge well of affection for him in the writing. This was never more apparent than in the episode where Wilson has to tell him that some of the platoon actually aren't very keen on doing drill or manoeuvres, that they would rather be doing something else than going on parade. Watching Arthur Lowe's touching performance at that point was like seeing a wartime barrage balloon slowly deflate. How could they possibly feel that way, he wondered aloud, when for him Home Guard activities were the highlight of his week, something he always looked forward to? And in that short scene we suddenly saw the whole dull life of a foolish, self-important middle-management man, with a not too sympathetic wife, who in late middle age had found excitement and purpose. It was a wonderful moment, and underscored the second brilliant aspect of the series – the casting.

At any given time there are hundreds of good actors in Britain, but in selecting the cast for *Dad's Army*, producer-director David Croft will never be bettered. Not one character was underwritten, and not one actor let his character down – to the extent that today all their little foibles are as familiar to us as those of our workmates or families.

The Private Godfrey character, played by Arnold Ridley (once well-known as the author of the successful play *The Ghost Train*), lived with his spinster sister Dolly, who occasionally made seedcakes; Pike (Ian Lavender), a total mother's boy, was too innocent to realise that Sergeant Wilson was sleeping with his mother (and may well also have been his father); Private Walker (James Beck), cunning and crooked, could get anything on the black market, often to Mainwaring's advantage; while Frazer (John Laurie) has at some time been imitated in every home in the country as the theatrically ghoulish Scottish undertaker. Then there was Bill Pertwee as the blustering air raid warden, and Clive Dunn as Corporal Jones with his cries of 'Don't panic!', while immediately doing exactly that. We've all met men like them, too.

Dad's Army was a period piece when first broadcast in the late Sixties, describing as it did a world which was even then largely forgotten, a time of shortages and rationing, social deference and small-town innocence. That it still works today, with a huge following in Australia and New Zealand as well as in the United Kingdom, is a testament to the authors' honesty and discipline in never taking their characters out of the world created for them. *Dad's Army* was about little people in a little place in an unusual time. And as such it's just about perfect.

Ken Dodd
Michael Coveney

Ken Dodd is a great British comedian and proud of it. Unquestionably the most extraordinary live performer I have ever seen, he represents a dying world of vaudeville, a music hall tradition that was for a time preserved in *The Good Old Days* on television and which can still be glimpsed in the annual pantomime. Frankie Howerd, Les Dawson and Tommy Cooper have all gone. Dodd is, or seems to be, quite literally unstoppable.

Dodd comes from the misty hinterland of English comedy, a mythical territory recorded in Donald McGill naughty postcards, a world of seaside boarding houses, funny foreigners, fearsome mother-in-laws, little men, large bosoms and sexual innuendos, with the distinct possibility of not coming up to scratch. Sex, after all, says Doddy, is what posh people have their coal delivered in.

Coal deliveries. Who remembers them now? Dodd for one. His father was a coal merchant in Knotty Ash, Liverpool, and he still lives in the family house, the house he was born in. You can hear the coal dust in his voice, often wheezy, and the occasional cough. He drives, or is driven, back to this house after most performances around the country. This background is so indelibly inscribed on his personality that he cannot bear to stay away. And besides, he dislikes the expense of staying in hotels. Like most great British comics of the old school, he is not only deeply patriotic, he is also slightly stingy.

Stereotypes are the lifeblood of a comic's material, especially the Northern comic's. Friendliness, for instance, is always relative. 'Had your tea?' you might say to a visitor. 'Pity, we've had ours.' This aggressive cheekiness is a Liverpudlian characteristic, and Dodd is nothing if not Scouse to the marrow, as were his two greatest heroes, Ted Ray and Arthur Askey.

What is his essential quality? He has been labelled a madcap jester, a celebratory comic, a surrealist clown and a dancing tailor's dummy escaped from Bedlam. But as anyone knows who has seen him 'live', he is quite different from how he comes across on television. The electricity of his stage presence is almost overwhelming, and he hits an audience with the force of a whirlwind.

But his appeal is, I believe, lodged in something even deeper and more atavistic than this. When a medieval jester turned up for a gig he would be carrying a pig's bladder. If he liked the look of someone in the audience, he would hit him over the head with it. What this was meant to signify is anyone's guess; perhaps that things could only start to improve.

Ken Dodd's pig's bladder substitute is the trademark tickling stick, which he waves over his head, pokes through his legs (from behind, Missus) or simply deposits on the hallowed boards. This is important, for Dodd is a master of ritual, a licensed fool, a timeless freak of nature with teeth that stick out and hair that he can pull into a comical cone. When he walked on like that for the first time in Glasgow he claims that a man in the third row swore loudly, shouted 'What a horrible sight!' and fell off his seat. He unleashes within an audience a combination of delight and fear, of anticipation and a sort of communal dread.

Ever undercutting any pretence at po-faced seriousness, Dodd is proud to tell us that his is an educational show. We'll go home afterwards and say, 'That taught me a lesson!' From his earliest days he kept a ledger of laughter, noting how loud and long the audience laughed, where the show sagged, where a new gag wasn't quite right, and so on. He was even interested in the comic theories of Aristotle and Freud. But the trouble with Aristotle and Freud, he observed, was that they never had to play second house on a Saturday night at the Glasgow Empire.

The really amazing thing about Dodd is that he never seems to lose his appetite for the job. In fact, it isn't really a job. It's a destiny. He wants to play every live theatre in the country, and he added one more to the list in the summer of 2002 when he appeared at the Open Air Theatre in Regent's Park. Here he was, he said, after more than forty years in the business, at the peak of his profession, admired of all his peers, performing in the middle of a field in a theatre that can't even afford a roof.

Over the years I have seen him on countless occasions – at the London Palladium, in Scarborough, Birmingham and Manchester, in Bromley, Windsor and Croydon, and always he refers to the theatre as 'this magnificent shed' and congratulates the audience on their new traffic system – 'They'll never find you now!' But while the material changes very slowly – he tries about six new gags every night – the show develops an orgiastic fervour that is entirely new and specific to each crowd of customers. I bumped into Dodd as he arrived at a stage door one evening and said that there was a full and expectant audience thronging the foyers. 'Good grief,' he replied, 'you mean to say there are 2,000 pregnant women out there?'

As a child, he went with his family to all the big variety houses in Liverpool and bought a booklet on how to become a ventriloquist. Leaving school at sixteen, he joined his father's business, but had already started entertaining at charity groups and Boy Scout gang shows. He made his debut at the Nottingham Empire in 1954, billing himself early on as either The Unpredictable Ken Dodd, or Professor Yaffle Chucklebutty, Operatic Tenor and Sausage Knotter.

The Diddymen, the Munchkin-style little folk who appear in the musical numbers, were inspired by his own small and plump uncle Jack, who wore a bowler hat. They work in the jam butty mines and snuff quarries of Knotty Ash and are impersonated by a crowd of small children whenever Dodd plays near enough to Liverpool for them to get home. Otherwise, these days, it's just the puppets, and his encounter with the inanimate Dicky Mint (other Diddymen are called Wee Hamish, Nigel Ponsonby-Smallpiece and so on) is a masterly ventriloquist's act: funny, eerie and strangely moving.

The big national breakthrough for Dodd was his London Palladium season of 1965,

A latter-day jester: Ken Dodd in 1965

when he packed the famous theatre for a record forty-two week run and had a number one hit in the charts, displacing his fellow Merseysiders, The Beatles. Twenty-four years later, in 1989, after two decades of television and radio fame, he appeared in a less welcome venue, Liverpool Crown Court, where he faced tax fraud charges. He was acquitted on all of them, but a melancholic picture had emerged.

Here was a wealthy man with no time for accountancy and even less to enjoy his fortune. He was enslaved to his talent. It's as simple as that. Like all great stage stars, he only comes alive in the spotlight. This is a mystery to people who have only ever seen him on television. For the fact is, Dodd is too big for the box, where he comes across as little more than a strange buffoon with slightly mouldy material.

There is a complicity between Dodd and a theatre audience which suggests we are all in for a long haul. He often says the usherettes will be taking orders for breakfast. Or that if you look under your seat you can find a will form. He will fix a woman in the front stalls with a threatening glare: 'This isn't television, Missus, you can't turn me off.' His rollercoaster show is as much about our endurance as about his: 'A feast of fun and a challenge to your kidneys.' Some of those Japanese shows go on for seven hours, he exclaims: 'We can do better than that!' But the melancholy keeps breaking through, not least when he sings 'Tears for Souvenirs' or 'Happiness', the sentimental songs that are his trademark.

In life, as on stage, Ken Dodd is Pagliacci reincarnate, the clown whose smile cracks into tears of yearning and despair. His fiancée of more than twenty years, Anita Boutin, died of a brain tumour in 1977. And his second long-term partner, Anne Jones, still loyally by his side at every performance – she also performs as a solo pianist and singer – has long since undergone fertility tests for the children he has never had. There is a poignancy that never fails to touch my heart when he sings 'Sonny Boy' to the lifeless little Dicky Mint doll.

'My life has been a series of tragedies,' he confides to the audience, 'culminating in tonight… Income Tax was invented two hundred years ago – at twopence in the pound; my trouble was I thought it still was… I've had problems, but nothing compared to those of the trapeze artist with loose bowels.'

Dodd's background was staunch old Labour. Ironically for one enduring the torture of that trial in his home town, his grandmother was Liverpool's first woman magistrate. Now, like most old-style comedians, Dodd is staunch old Tory. He admired Mrs Thatcher and feels deeply that she gave the nation back its pride. And now he himself occupies a special place in our culture. He has several honorary citations and an OBE ('One Boiled Egg'). And he'll not give in, not until we do, or he drops. It's a fight to the end.

The Ealing Comedies
Alexander Walker

'Cry God for Ealing, Balcon and St George.' That's how it might have gone. Sir Michael (Mick) Balcon, the head of Ealing Studios for almost thirty years, wasn't a man for war cries, however. His love of England resounded in his heart, not in his eardrums: the crack of bat hitting ball was the only sound of battle he enjoyed. His last words to me, spoken as I left his country house after Sunday afternoon tea one day in 1959, when Ealing Studios had shut down, were ones of sorrow that he wouldn't live to see the fine willow row he'd planted a few years earlier grow into cricket bats.

Like the man himself, his films spoke for Middle England, or rather (among the thirty films he produced from 1938 on) the half-dozen did that we call 'Ealing comedies'. Appositely, the year Ealing ceased production, 1958, was also the year R F Delderfield (best known for his West End hit *Worm's Eye View*) published his novel *The Dreaming Suburb*. Ealing films, I've often thought, were the dreams those suburbs dreamed: they were the fantasies that the middle classes let loose in the hours when their respectability was off guard.

Yet the Ealing comedies were rooted in the shabby-heroic realities of post-war Britain: a land of bombed sites, spivs, rationing, men and women demobbed from war work or the front line, politically radical but patriotically conservative, and Whitehall bureaucrats still reluctant to surrender their power over the people. Ealing had made its wartime name as a realist cinema with docudramas like *Ships with Wings*, *San Demetrio London* and *For Those in Peril*. Peace provided the opportunity to continue the war by other, gentler means.

Passport to Pimlico defied the Men from the Ministry (Naunton Wayne and Basil Radford, of course) by a unilateral declaration of independence (long before devolution) and setting up an independent dukedom in SW1, where Stanley Holloway was prime minister (for a day and a night anyhow). *Whisky Galore*, with its islanders outwitting their (English) Home Guard commander (Radford again) to plunder the wrecked ship of its cargo of spirits, enlisted the sneaking British sympathy for a certain class of law-breaking that was victimless. Similarly, *The Lavender Hill* mob gave those who dared – the commuting classes – a vision of quick riches that would have to wait another fifty years for the National Lottery to make it a weekly reality, and then wouldn't be half so exciting as a chase up and down the Eiffel Tower. Even where victims existed, they were eccentric ones. Dennis Price in *Kind Hearts and Coronets* worked his way through all eight of the d'Ascoyne line of toffs, one by one, all of them looking like Alec Guinness even in drag, as if he were coolly pulling together some loose threads on a modern Bayeux Tapestry of mass carnage. And *The Man in the White Suit* released other passions about 'them' and 'us', particularly the Luddite mistrust of Big Business.

Overleaf: *Alec Guinness and Stanley Holloway in* The Lavender Hill Mob *(1951)*

Again and again, Ealing's comedies celebrated the British love for all things old: old puffers (*The Titfield Thunderbolt*), old tubs (*The Maggie*), old piers (*Barnacle Bill*), old crocks (*Genevieve*, which, though made at Rank's Pinewood Studios, was originally an Ealing project). Ealing Studios were based on Ealing Green, North London, and that leafy and herbivorous address suggested – if only in the mind's eye – the seductive perspective of an England that Mick Balcon and his team of writers and directors treasured like a bit of the National Trust. They oversaw a land much like a large village common, where everyone knew his place and getting above yourself in such a community, even if you'd invented a white suit that never wore out, never needed cleaning, carried risks of upsetting the liberal paternalism of settled life.

Upset it had to be, of course, usually by some quixotic individual (Margaret Rutherford in *Passport to Pimlico*, Alastair Sim as the cartoonist whose fantasies become gangster reality in *Hue and Cry*); but the harmony of consensus politics was always restored. It was a storm in a teacup, never a typhoon. The 'little man' ruled – in the last reel anyhow – as modestly heroic as he'd looked in Straub's famous pocket cartoons in the still rationed newsprint. Small was beautiful. *Whisky Galore* was retitled *Tight Little Island* for US audiences; for once, the sea-change was apt. Ealing's outlook was insular, little and uptight where the more dangerous passions were concerned.

Like sex and violence. In such things, Balcon shared Middle England's reticence. Yes, *The Ladykillers* postulated social disorder, even serial murder, but it was the innocent and sweet old lady (Katie Johnson) who finished up acquiring the loot (and tipping a pound note to the street artist who'd crayoned Winston Churchill's portrait on the flagstones), while the mutual immolation of her would-be murderers was 'just the ticket', a guilt-free placebo in a land that still hanged its murderers. Sex, though, was the great untreatable on screen, just as it was still the great unspeakable in public. Story conferences at Ealing – self-deprecatingly advertising itself on billboards, in a perfect English understatement, as simply 'The Home of Good Pictures' – preferred to speak of the 'love interest', and not much of that either: romance from the neck up, not below the waist. Kenneth Tynan dismissively spoke of Ealing heroes as 'men who communicate with their women mainly by post-cards'. But Balcon saw nothing reprehensible in that; and Britain agreed with him, or at least the male kingdom did.

Now we look back and perhaps the word 'quaint' comes to our lips. If so, it would be as unjust as it is unkind. Ealing Studios may have produced comfort food for Middle England that sat well with the national stomach in a nation that, possibly for the last time in its modern history, saw itself as a unitary community. One may blame the films for their conservatism, for their punishment of individual pushiness, their love of communal cosiness, veneration of consensus politics and toleration of subversiveness only so long as it was benign, comic and ultimately hurt no one. Ealing was, like Camelot, only a brief moment in cultural history, which ended as a new, thrusting and liberated generation came of age in the late 1950s. But, for that moment, studio and nation were at ease with each other. The plaque put on the wall at Ealing Green when the studios were sold to the BBC says it all: 'Here during a quarter of a century were made many films projecting Britain and the British character.' The claim could scarcely have been more modestly assembled, or more truthfully made.

Fawlty Towers
Iain Johnstone

The most amazing thing about Fawlty Towers was that anyone was able to find it. The hotel nearly always masqueraded under a pseudonym, from 'Fatty Owls' to 'Wart Towels', from 'Flay Otters' to 'Flowery Twats'.

It was all part of John Cleese's art and artfulness. Having spent three years with the *Monty Python* troupe trying to avoid punchlines, he chose to end his signature series with both a verbal one and a visual one.

So how did it come about, this unlikely but quintessentially British comedy, which in 2000 was voted the best television programme of the twentieth century? In the spring of 1973 Jimmy Gilbert, BBC TV's Head of Comedy, invited John Cleese to lunch at a long-forgotten restaurant called The Gun Room in West London. Gilbert knew that Cleese was restive about appearing in any more *Monty Python* shows (indeed he pulled out of the programme that year) and was anxious to keep the BBC's most iconoclastic talent sweet. He was prepared to give him a free hand to do any series he liked. Did John have any ideas?

Yes, as it happened, he did. He was always annoyed about the shortcomings of service in the various hotels he had stayed in on locations over the years and he wanted to get his own back. He would like to play a barely repressed, henpecked hotelier called Basil (named after the street where he lived). Gilbert gulped down his glass of Riesling. How was he going to tell his BBC bosses that the anarchic Cleese proposed to turn the comedy clock back twenty years with a show that sounded like *Crossroads* with gags? What he didn't know – and few have – was that John had already prototyped his invention.

On 12 October 1970 London Weekend Television recorded 'Come and Lie Down' – an episode in the comedy series *Six Dates with Barker*. Ronnie Barker, Cleese's colleague from *The Frost Report* – 'He's upper class so he looks down on me' – played a psychiatrist, a profession that greatly interested John (and would, of course, provide the premise and title of one of the most celebrated episodes of *Fawlty Towers*). Michael Bates appeared as a first-time patient, so intimidated by the prospect of being analysed that he initially pretended he was a gasman who had come to read the meter. Undoubtedly, Cleese had crafted the Bates character to be an early Basil, a tall man with a moustache and angular body language who, in the course of his session, goes from lapel-clutching bullying – 'I'll smash your face in' – to folding up in self-pitying despair. His crucial description of himself was: 'I may be odd, but in an English sort of way, acceptably odd.'

LWT later assigned Cleese six *Doctor at Large* scripts. John had studied law and didn't know much about hospital life, so he had the ingenuity to move the plots to places that

---

Overleaf: *John Cleese as Basil Fawlty and Andrew Sachs as Manuel in* Fawlty Towers

were familiar – like small, inefficient hotels. Thus in April 1971 Barry Evans, playing Dr Upton, is forced to check into the Bella Vista Hotel when he takes up a post as a locum. From the first ping of the desk bell (a comic device used so cleverly by Buck Henry in *The Graduate*) Upton is in Fawltyland. Little old ladies look on as Mr Clifford, the proprietor, ignores him, being summoned from the desk by his henpecking wife. 'Why should I do the sprouts?' we hear him ask cravenly. 'No Ill Feeling' was largely set in the dining room of the hotel where Fawlty was to have his finest hours. Timothy Bateson played Clifford in a quieter, Buster Keatonesque fashion, even wearing an apron, but with the barb of the Cleese dialogue. When offered the choice of sausages or a kipper for breakfast, a rushed Upton asks 'Would a kipper be quicker?' and Clifford snaps back 'How quick can a kipper be?'

But the fundamental inspiration for Basil Fawlty was one Donald Sinclair, proprietor of the Gleneagles Hotel, Torquay. Here was a man who was *unacceptably* odd in an English sort of way. His *modus operandi* was less to serve his guests than to boss them. The Pythons stayed there on location. One day Eric Idle came back from filming and asked Sinclair if he had seen his bag, which he had forgetfully left in the hall. 'Yes, I put it behind there,' snapped the proprietor, pointing to a stone wall some fifty yards away in a field. Eric was incredulous. 'Why?' 'It might have had a bomb in it,' said Sinclair, although this was not at a time of terrorist activity in Britain, nor was Eric Idle in the habit of blowing up hotels. Sinclair would parade the dining room like a sergeant-major, and once stopped at the *Python* table, staring deliberately at the American, Terry Gilliam, who was eating peas off his knife. 'That's not the way we do things in this country,' he informed the entire room.

I spoke to Rosemary Harrison, who actually worked as a waitress in the hotel in the summer of 1973. It was a necessary element of her hotel management course and her sister Christine came down from Scotland with her husband and child to stay for ten days. On the second night they were having a drink in the bar after dinner. Sinclair was serving, but at 9.00 pm he pulled down the grill and announced that the bar was now closed because he was going to bed. Some guests complained. The response of their host was: 'Tough.' But the most outrageous moment in Christine's stay was the night when Sinclair, in his brochure, advertised a Friday night dinner dance. The Gleneagles was a four-star hotel, much bigger than Fawlty Towers, and unknowing young couples from Torquay, many in evening dress, came to join the residents in what promised to be an enjoyable evening. After dinner they waited and waited… and waited. But no musicians, or music of any kind, arrived. Bolder guests began to complain to Donald Sinclair. His response was to leave the restaurant and come back with a gramophone which he plonked, unplugged, onto the floor. In his habitual manner, he then stomped off to bed, failing to provide any records.

Had John Cleese and his then wife, Connie Booth, known of this last incident when they sat down to write the first six episodes of *Fawlty Towers*, it is doubtful if they could have included it. It simply beggared belief. The brilliance of their scripts was that each had an internal logic to it, while Donald clearly had none at all.

There were only twelve episodes of *Fawlty Towers* in all, and more than a three-year gap between the sixth one –'The Germans' (one of that select group of comic inspirations to have bequeathed to the language a phrase of almost proverbial force: 'Don't mention the war') – and the seventh – 'Communication Problems' (the one where Basil, against Sybil's dictate, puts a bet on a horse). Cleese and Booth had the discipline not only to hone each episode to perfection, but also to stop well before the series ran out of steam. As a result, not only is each of the episodes a classic of its kind, but twenty-eight years after the first one was screened in September 1975 the cast still benefit from the repeat fees, foreign television sales, videos and DVDs throughout the world – plus, more importantly, the lingering fame.

But one performer did not share in this good fortune – the actress Cleese and Booth originally approached to play Sybil. One of the many strengths of *Fawlty Towers* is its impeccable ensemble playing, and it is characteristic of their thoroughgoing professionalism that John and Connie should have taken as much care over the casting as over the scripts. Eleven of the twelve episodes (the exception is 'The Health Inspector') are pretty much predicated on Basil hiding something from Sybil, but as they read through their early drafts, they realised that it would be inappropriate for Connie herself to play Fawlty's wife. John was in his early thirties and was going to play a maniac in his fifties; Connie was too young and too beautiful and better engaged as Polly, the maid. Not only that – their marriage was about to hit rough waters, and they were to separate before the second series.

Alan Ayckbourn's *The Norman Conquests* was playing in London's Globe Theatre at the time when the search for Sybil was getting desperate. The play had a distinguished cast, most of whom were to become even more distinguished: Felicity Kendal OBE, Penny Keith OBE, Sir Michael Gambon and Sir Tom Courtenay. But it was the woman playing Norman's wife that Cleese was interested in, an actress called Bridget Turner. John offered her the part of Sybil Fawlty and gave her a couple of scripts. But she didn't find them very funny and turned him down. The rest is Prunella Scales and history.

The other casualty was the hotel itself. The exteriors had been filmed, not in Torquay, but in Buckinghamshire at the Woodbury Grange Country Club. When such establishments went out of fashion it was turned into an Indian restaurant which, after a few lean years, mysteriously burnt down.

But the spirit of Basil will linger for a long, long time.

Flanders and Swann
Adam Hart-Davis

When I were a lad, my dad used to take me before Christmas to a show in the West End of London, and I still remember a few of the ones we saw. *Christmas Magic and Fun* was OK, but the performance I recall most vividly and with most affection was *At the Drop of a Hat*, which appeared in the late 1950s. I don't know where the name came from, but I do know my father was being fairly heroic in taking me, since he had already seen the show twice. However, it was an excellent choice, since it's still clear in my memory almost fifty years on.

There was this thin, bespectacled, rather bird-like man who played the piano, and a fat chap with a beard and a wheelchair who sang songs, and I thought they were utterly wonderful. We bought the recording of the show – one of those new-fangled 'long-playing microgroove' things with all the songs on one record – and at home on the farm in Oxfordshire I played it again and again until I knew every word.

I am not a great singer. When I sing people around me tend to adopt pained expressions and leave the room, or ask me to stop. Nevertheless, I do like to practise in the shower, and occasionally at parties I am allowed to give a rendering of 'Misalliance', which is perhaps my favourite of all Flanders and Swann's songs – a simple tune, faint sexual overtones and a brilliant idea conveyed in clever words.

The song describes the fate of a honeysuckle and a bindweed that fall in love, but are doomed because they twine in opposite directions. That is the basic idea, and about the extent of the sex. But the words are lovely:

Said the right-handed Honeysuckle / to the left-handed Bindweed:
'Oh let us get married / if our parents don't mind; we'd
Be loving and inseparable, / inextricably entwined; we'd
Live happily ever after,' / said the Honeysuckle to the Bindweed.

But the honeysuckle's parents do mind – 'the Bindweeds,' they cry, 'are inferior stock' – and so the couple consider eloping:

Said the anti-clockwise Bindweed / to the clockwise Honeysuckle:
'We'd better start saving, / many a mickle maks a muckle,
Then run away for our honeymoon / and hope that our luck'll
Take a turn for the better,' / said the Bindweed to the Honeysuckle.

Michael Flanders (left) and Donald Swann (right)

(The last line has to be sung rather quickly). But the plot thickens, a passing bee gives them gloomy advice, and the story has a tragic ending. The rhymes are perhaps not as knowingly sophisticated as the best of Tom Lehrer, a performer with whom Flanders and Swann are sometimes compared. But the apparent simplicity of the Flanders words and the ideas in the songs made them enormously appealing to me. I could appreciate almost everything they sang about without any knowledge of politics or literature or fashion – indeed, they had a gift for mocking things fashionable, such as the so-called labour-saving devices in 'Too Many Cookers', or ovens 'with an eye-level grill … so that the hot fat can squirt straight into your eyes'.

One of their more risqué songs, 'Madeira, M'dear', included some of the most enjoyable syllepses I can recall:

> And he said as he hastened to put out the cat,
> The wine, his cigar and the lamps,
> 'Have some Madeira, m'dear!'

And later, when the girl has realised her mistake:

When he asked: 'What in heaven…?' she made no reply,
Up her mind and a dash for the door.

Some lyricists use tricks of the English language like sledgehammers – Bob Hope and Bing Crosby's 'like Webster's dictionary, we're Morocco bound' is a great line, but definitely in your face. Flanders and Swann built their joyous subtleties so deeply into the songs that often I simply did not notice the jokes the first few times I heard them, but then conversely they have remained enjoyable ever since.

Michael Flanders and Donald Swann met at Westminster school in 1936, but did not really start working together until after the war, during which Flanders had caught polio after his ship was torpedoed. As a result, he was confined to a wheelchair for the rest of his life. Flanders was, as he said, 'the big one with the beard who writes the words and does most of the talking', while Swann wrote the music and both of them – 'for want of a better word' – sang. *At the Drop of a Hat* was their first independent professional revue, and it made their names.

In *At the Drop of a Hat* Donald Swann was allowed to sing one song on his own, which on stage was set up by Flanders with a sneer: 'Donald will now sing a song in modern Greek.' Swann did indeed sing, and the song, '*Kokoraki*', was like a Greek version of 'Old MacDonald Had a Farm'. When Swann came to the end of verse five, Flanders wheeled his chair out to the front with relief plain on his face, and was about to announce the next piece when Swann started on verse six. Flanders retreated with resignation. This happened twice more, and the audience were hooting with laughter.

When Swann finally stopped, Flanders turned to him and asked whether he had completely finished. Swann: 'I left out the last eight verses.' Flanders: 'Let's have it in full some time, alternating with the Ring Cycle! What on earth is it that goes "Tsou-tsou" anyway?' Swann: '*To petinari* – the little chicks.' Flanders caustically to the audience: 'Have you ever heard a chick going "Tsou-tsou"?'

These little snatches of dialogue, or Flanders monologue, were an integral part of the performance, and set the songs in the context of a stage relationship – Swann the unworldly intellectual, Flanders urbane, bluff and trenchant – that made them all the more memorable. Occasionally they sang real duets, such as 'The Reluctant Cannibal', in which Flanders styled himself chief assistant to the assistant chief, and Swann was his son, who had decided that 'Eating people is wrong'. The arguments Flanders uses to try to bring him round are wonderful: 'Have you been talking to one of your mothers again?' 'If the Ju-Ju had meant us not to eat people, he wouldn't have made us of meat.' The pay-off was harder-edged, a reminder that, for all their cosmopolitan charm, the songs were being sung against the background of the Cold War and the nuclear arms race: 'You might as well say "Don't *fight* people!"'

Some of the songs were just plain silly, like 'A Gnu' ('Oh g-no, g-no, g-no, I'm a G-nu'). Others had rich resonances with life as we know it – such as 'The Gasman Cometh' and especially 'A Transport of Delight':

Along the Queen's great highway / I drive my merry load
At twenty miles per hour / in the middle of the road.
We like to drive in convoys / we're most gregarious
The big six-wheeler / scarlet-painted / London Transport
Diesel-engined / ninety-seven horsepower omnibus!

And above all, or perhaps below all, the song that everyone remembers was 'The Hippopotamus', with its resounding chorus with which in the theatre the audience needed little encouragement to join in:

Mud! Mud! Glorious mud!
Nothing quite like it for cooling the blood!
So, follow me, follow, down to the hollow,
And there let us wallow in glo-orious mud.

In *At the Drop of a Hat* Flanders sat slightly hippo-like in his wheelchair; Swann sat hunched over the piano. The only other thing on the stage was a standard lamp. In the *Daily Telegraph* W A Darlington wrote: 'It is an astonishing entertainment. When the curtain rises, your natural reaction is to wonder how they will keep things going for the whole evening. But once their insidious brand of lunacy gets hold of you, you believe they might easily keep things going for a week if they wanted.'

In fact, they kept things going for years. They toured their shows all over the world, and recorded a studio album, *The Bestiary of Flanders and Swann*, which added to their celebrated hippo and gnu a cast of other all-too-human animals, including a day-dreaming sloth, a chronically boring boar and a bottle-nosed whale with the 'flu. In 1963 their second revue, *At the Drop of Another Hat* (in which the hippo makes an encore appearance, now weighed down by the burdens of marriage and fatherhood), opened to great acclaim in London, and they continued performing together regularly until 1967. Recently a CD collection of their complete recordings was issued, bringing to a new generation of admirers their uniquely British brand of gentle, finely observed and inconspicuously crafted social satire.

There is a coda to my memories of Flanders and Swann, whom I never met (Michael Flanders died in 1975, Donald Swann in 1994). Apart from Flanders himself, one of the finest performers of their songs was Ian Wallace, a small man with a huge voice. In the summer of 2002 I was filming in Highgate, wearing a seventeenth-century costume and being towed along in a carriage. During a break in the filming an elderly gent came tottering across the road with a stick to tell me how much he enjoyed my television programmes, and introduced himself as Ian Wallace. What a pleasure it was to meet the man who above all others was a living link to that incomparable duo and the songs of that never-forgotten Christmas revue of my childhood.

Stephen Fry
Oliver James

'Oscar Wilde teaches one to take the serious things in life trivially and the trivial things seriously. That's ultimately my attitude,' Stephen Fry told me in 1988 when I interviewed him for a TV programme. A lifelong depressive, Fry has had good reason to want to distance himself from, and to lighten up, his true feelings. In the process, he has produced some of the cleverest jokes and *aperçus* of our age.

He is rated at the very top by his peers. John Lloyd, the TV comedy producer, once told me that 'if there is such a thing as a genius, Stephen is it'. That is no mean compliment coming from Lloyd – his curriculum vitae consists of *The Hitchhiker's Guide to the Galaxy*, *Not the Nine o'Clock News*, *Spitting Image* and *Blackadder*; those are the only programmes he ever produced, all of them won BAFTA awards, and after he had finished *Blackadder* he retired from television.

Part of Lloyd's admiration comes from Fry's ability to shine in an unusually wide range of genres. He made a fortune in the 1980s by writing the lyrics for the musical *Me and My Girl*, following in the footsteps of one of his two great comic heroes, P G Wodehouse. In print, his brief period of journalism was widely feted and resulted in bestselling compilation books. His novel *The Liar* was hugely successful, as was his autobiography, the title of which, *Moab Is My Washpot*, is characteristic in its combination of allusiveness and eccentricity. His comic sketch series with Hugh Laurie on the BBC (*A Bit of Fry and Laurie*) may not have distinguished itself so clearly from the competition as some of his work, but it never failed to amuse. The same is true of his numerous appearances on BBC Radio 4, most notably as a very competitive competitor on *Just a Minute*. But on top of all that, he has put in some powerful as well as hugely entertaining film and television drama performances, such as his depiction of Jeeves in *Jeeves and Wooster* (a reprise, with Hugh Laurie, of the Wodehouse roles first realised on television by Dennis Price and Ian Carmichael); his *Blackadder* cameos as, among others, the obsequious Elizabethan courtier Lord Melchett and his cannon-feeding World War One descendant General Melchett; and the title role in Brian Gilbert's 1997 film of the life of Oscar Wilde.

Along with Wodehouse, Wilde is absolutely central to Fry's humour, a soul-brother in his love of paradox. (Fry once began a magazine column with the words: 'The world is divided into two sorts of people: those who divide the world into two sorts of people and those who do not. I fall resolutely into the latter category.') Along with a certain levity that is neither facetious nor flippant, what both of his idols share is a love of great cleverness, but cleverness so clever as not to be attention-seeking. Although Fry is very competitive, he is also a sensitive chap; his ultimate purpose is not to make you feel thick or to be malicious. Like the work of his heroes, his wit contains a profound humanism, a sympathy for every character's predicament.

So what are the roots of this prodigious comedic talent? I believe they lie in Fry's difficult childhood and life. Adopting the light touch of a Wilde or a Wodehouse creates a buffer against a nagging, massive, irrational self-hatred. 'My achievements have been driven by a fear of inadequacy and unpopularity,' he told me. 'As an adolescent I was shy and awkward. I had an appalling body image, thought of myself as a quite revolting specimen and still do to some extent – I think most people or a lot of people do.' Do they? His view of his sexual eligibility drips with self-loathing: 'I don't think of myself as an oil painting – oil slick would be closer. The fact that I don't inflict myself on women is the greatest favour I can do them.'

Fry was '90 per cent gay' before he became famously celibate in the mid-Eighties, something he first revealed in his interview with me. Like about half of all gay men, he had a difficult relationship with his father and was close to his mother. A scientist and businessman, Alan Fry was apt to find fault with everything his son did. 'I always found myself implacably opposed to him,' Stephen recalled. 'There was a lot of tension and rivalry. He knew I was bright and therefore he was very irritated. He scared the living daylights out of me until I was twenty… He frowned at anything I did with any degree of competence.' This attitude was still detectable in comments Alan made about his son in 1991: 'I sometimes feel like saying to him: "stop doing this pappy and ephemeral stuff on the box and get down to some serious writing". Stephen spends a lot of energy doing things that aren't worthy of him.'

Given that Stephen was subjected to this negativity throughout childhood, it is perhaps hardly surprising that he has such a low opinion of himself. But crucially, he has consistently refused to admit its effect, maintaining an admirable if excessive loyalty towards his father, who has said, 'I'm sure if I were attacked Stephen'd be a tiger unleashed in my defence'. But there is a heavy price to be paid for this loyalty. Because he cannot properly acknowledge the anger he feels, it ends up being directed back against himself – becomes depression.

Fry is aware, however, that he dislikes authority and that this is linked to his attitude to his father: 'I do associate all authority with my father,' he told me. Anti-authoritarianism is another reason he admires Oscar Wilde: 'He challenged received wisdoms and used words to subvert the status quo – reversals like "Work is the curse of the drinking classes" and "Nature imitates art".' Fry adored such artifice and used it to help him cope. Like his idol, he constantly engaged in impostures.

When I spoke with him in 1988, and for many years afterwards, he rarely if ever stopped assuming personae, which may be why he told me his greatest fear was 'being found out – most men live in fear of a nameless "being found out"'. Paradoxically, like many actor-comedians, he felt most real when pretending to be someone else: 'A fiction is the best way to be true,' he said. Perhaps when you are small, pretending to be someone else is a good way of escaping criticism – if you pretend to be someone else then you

---

Overleaf: *Stephen Fry (right) with Hugh Laurie in* A Bit of Fry and Laurie

cannot be attacked for being you. Of course, it is over-simple to reduce all of Fry's work to a mere attempt to evade his father. There is such a thing as healthy playfulness as well. But there is a thin line between a child believing in its imaginary friends, a novelist locked into the fictional lives of his characters and a conviction that you are actually someone else, not just acting them, or, as Wodehouse always joked when talking about someone who is mad, claiming you are a poached egg. There is no evidence that Fry has ever crossed that line, but the mental pressures under which he was operating were very publicly revealed in 1995 by his notorious disappearance during the West End run of Simon Gray's play *Cell Mates*, in which he was starring opposite Rik Mayall.

Whether or not, as Fry has subsequently claimed, that episode marked a turning point in his psychological history, it is interesting to see how much his state of mind may have changed in recent years. Back in 1988, he told me that, although he had been 90 per cent gay, he was now sure he was heterosexual. He said he 'feared depending on others or them depending on me', but he also said he would like, in theory, to get married. By contrast, today he is certain he is gay and his life has been hugely stabilised by sharing it with a partner. Such dependence may mean he is more himself and happier, and that, in turn, may mean he has less need to make light of his life. He may become less funny as a result – though there is precious little sign of it as yet – but if that is our loss, we would surely never begrudge him the gain.

The Good Life
Jonathon Porritt

My mum and dad loved *The Good Life*. Like many men of a certain age, my dad, I suspect, particularly loved tuning in to Felicity Kendal once a week, though my mother was reassuringly free of any similar attraction to Richard Briers. And I rather liked it too: all that commendable self-sufficiency, the wholesome lifestyle and quite improbable closeness to nature – and all in a Surbiton back garden. As an avowed greenie from the early 1970s onwards, for me this was as close as television ever got (apart from the evergreen David Attenborough, who was hard at work creating the legend even then) to addressing some of the issues about which I was already insufferably earnest.

And Barbara and Tom could have done earnest for Britain. Were it not for the fact that the sitcom format required at least one joke or witty aside every thirty seconds, I wonder just how good the 'good life' would really have looked to people. Not that we saw too much of them at it, but the hours between the jokes – out in the back garden, in backbreaking labour, in all weathers – seemed far from idyllic. Anyone with even a lingering notion that the good life was for them would instantly have signed up to a life of sybaritic debauchery. My mum would occasionally rub my nose in this high church ecological correctness: 'Sounds just like you, darling – are you advising them on the script?'

It's amazing to think back to that time, but there really was a burgeoning self-sufficiency movement, with people like John Seymour advocating a return to the land as a way of escaping the urban rat-race. Really quite sensible people decided to go and live in communes, speaking eloquently of liberating themselves from the shackles of shallow consumerism. Despite the earnestness, I suspect Tom and Barbara must have served as inspirational role-models to countless weary souls seeking meaning and inner tranquillity through what we now call 'downshifting'.

I have to admit that this vision of an alternative life never quite did it for me. Not only did all plants and flowers have an irritating tendency to give up the ghost the moment I laid fingers on them, but it was already apparent that DIY was not where I was destined to make any impact on the world. There is only so much bodging ineptitude that one can overcome to make a go of self-sufficiency. Indeed, 'do *not* do it yourself' was a dictum that came to me quite naturally from the moment at the age of six when my very first treehouse collapsed, bringing me back down to earth with a plummeting sense of dread to which I attribute a residual vertigo forty-six years on.

But Tom and Barbara were very good indeed at making do and mending. Pigsties, looms, automatic feeders for assorted livestock, raised beds, gazebos, cucumber frames –

Overleaf: *Surbiton quartet: Richard Briers, Felicity Kendal, Paul Eddington and Penelope Keith*

you name it, they made it. With all this cash going out the door (there was, after all, very little barter going on in Surbiton in those days), they always seemed to be on the verge of bankruptcy, selling just enough summer fruits or manky leeks to keep themselves in seeds, bailer twine and goat pellets. I'm afraid I was cynical enough on occasions to suspect that Tom had stashed enough from his previous 'real world' existence as an advertising artist to keep the wolves of debt from his self-sufficient doorway.

But more than half the pleasure of *The Good Life* lay in the other half of the quartet around which it all revolved – Margot and Jerry, the neighbours, exemplifying as they did Surbiton man and woman. Margot was almost magnificent in her irrepressible snobbery, her vanity, her unashamed delight in the joys of shopping. Not just keeping up with the Joneses, but constantly beating them down in an orgy of conspicuous consumption, was pretty much her life's work.

Which must have made Barbara a more than vexing neighbour for her. On the one hand, Barbara offered no competition at all – indeed, she must have been contemptible to Margot in her refusal even to acknowledge that there was a serious competition going on out there, day in day out. On the other hand, Barbara and Tom were clearly a dreadful blight on the neighbourhood, dragging down 'the tone' with their ramshackle sheds, noisy pigs and the kind of sartorial style that one wouldn't wish on one's mother-in-law.

Margot was also a dreadful bully – of all and sundry, but particularly of her long-suffering spouse. However, even as Jerry did what he was told, he maintained a remarkably resilient independence. He was clearly in love with Barbara, in an elegantly inconsequential kind of way, and the mixture of contempt, envy and friendship that he felt for Tom made for some interesting chemistry. And he got as close to accurately interpreting their world as any of them: 'Come on, Tom, don't give me any more of that self-righteous self-sufficiency – allotments are simply places where men go to sit so they don't have to talk to their wives.'

Little did we know it then, but in this remarkably simple dynamic lay an emerging clash of cultures (or civilisations even). Margot and Jerry stood up true for unabashed

Life satisfaction? Tom and Barbara get close to nature

materialism, instant gratification and the right to remain fun-loving but superficial in almost all circumstances. Quality of life through quantity of cash. I shop, therefore I am. By contrast, Tom and Barbara flew the flag for voluntary simplicity, the dignity of manual labour and the right to remain unbearably superior even in dire poverty.

I need hardly point out that Margot and Jerry have won hands down. Even as the world has come to a grudging awareness that we really can't go on like this much longer, so grave is the environmental crisis, the wheels of our consumer-driven economy spin ever faster. A decade of me-first, why-wait-till-tomorrow gratification followed hard on the heels of the 1992 Earth Summit in Rio de Janeiro as if it had never taken place at all. Today's Tom and Barbara lookalikes find themselves staring out in disbelief at a world that seems to get crazier every year, even more wasteful, even more self-destructive.

But maybe the shades of Tom and Barbara will have the last laugh yet. Just consider these two fascinating insights into the collective psyche of modern Britain – both culled from an official government paper on 'Life Satisfaction' published by the Cabinet Office in November 2002. First, the fact that since 1970 GDP per head of population has almost doubled, while people's assessment of their 'life satisfaction' has remained static. This is the naked truth no politician dare give voice to: that even as we get richer (in terms of per capita income), we don't get any happier – as millions of Margots and Jerries so plainly demonstrate as they flog their lives out on the treadmill of consumerism.

And second, the graph below:

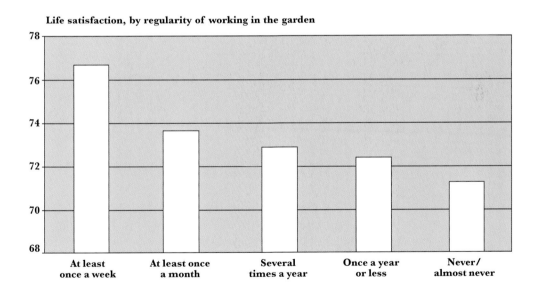

Life satisfaction, by regularity of working in the garden

the definitive proof that Tom and Barbara really did have access to a deeper, earthbound wisdom – though of course their particular devotion to gardening warranted a different classification, in terms of 'all day, every day', taking them and their good life right off the scale.

The Goons
Fergus Fleming

In the mid-1950s Britain was in serious trouble. Crackling over the radio waves came the news that the 'constabule' on duty outside Number 10 Downing Street had been struck on the nut with a handbasin. 'An' when I come three… er, to… the building 'ad gorn.' This was a crisis. The nation needed men of stout heart to save it. Men like Eccles. 'Women like Eccles too,' objected Spike Milligan.

'The Theft of Number 10 Downing Street' was just one of many *Goon Show* masterpieces that glued Britons to their radios for half an hour every Monday evening for six months of every year from 1951 to 1960. Relentless in its wit, innovative in its use of sound effects and, in its surrealism, unlike anything that had ever appeared before, the programme gripped the nation. At its peak, more than four million households tuned in to the BBC Home Service to hear Harry Secombe welcome them to the 'Brand new, all-leather *Goon Show*!' What might happen next was anyone's guess. The only certainty was that Ned Seagoon would suffer further misfortunes at the hands of Eccles, Bluebottle, Bloodnok, Grytpype-Thynne, Moriarty and the two squabbling pensioners, Henry Crun and Minnie Bannister.

The Goons had their unlikely origin in North Africa. It was here, during World War Two, that trumpeter and singer Terence Alan ('Spike') Milligan met pay clerk Harry Secombe, with whom he shared the same ridiculous sense of humour. On being demobbed, they made their way to London's Windmill Theatre, where they discovered two soulmates: Michael Bentine and Peter Sellers. While pursuing their separate stage careers – Milligan made his debut on *Opportunity Knocks* in 1949 – the four held regular after-work sessions from which emerged a concept for a radio show. After two years and countless revisions it was finally accepted by the BBC. The first episode was broadcast in May 1951. Called *Those Crazy People* because the programmers said nobody would understand the word 'Goon' ('Who are these Go-ons?' asked one man), the show was initially just a random sequence of gags scripted by Bentine and Milligan. After two series, however, Bentine left the team – of his own accord but perhaps also because of creative differences. At the same time Milligan decided to give the gags a plot, and in 1952 the *Goon Show* came into its own. For this was not a plot in the normal sense of the word, but a string of nonsense held together by something that could only just be called logic. In Milligan's world anything was possible – NAAFI canteens could fly, Napoleon's piano could be rowed across the English Channel and, of course, Number 10 Downing Street could be stolen.

It was Sellers who sold the Goons. As Bloodnok, Bluebottle, Grytpype-Thynne, Henry Crun and others, he created an unforgettable repertoire of accents which, two generations later, were still the stuff of schoolboy imitation. (Prince Charles once went live as a very creditable Bluebottle.) Fellow performers were amazed, if not alarmed, at the ease with which he assumed his roles: Secombe said it was little short of terrifying to watch him become Thynne; and Milligan stood in genuine awe of his abilities. But if Sellers was the salesman, Milligan was the man who manufactured the goods. It was he who created not only the whole lunatic edifice but the characters who inhabited it. The Hon. Hercules Grytpype-Thynne, suede-voiced, upper-class scrounger, was modelled on a man he had met on an aeroplane, who spoke grandiosely of millions of pounds, yet had string for cufflinks and a large hole in his sock through which could be seen a patch of blackened skin. ('I think he left owing the cabin crew something,' Milligan recalled.) Eccles was based on Goofy, one of Milligan's childhood favourites, but a Goofy who had evolved into a basic form of *homo sapiens* with a peculiar immunity to reason. Major Dennis Bloodnok was every corrupt, wife-snatching, gambling officer Milligan had met during his upbringing in India. As for Bluebottle, he was an unfortunate man with a red beard and a squeaky voice who arrived at the stage door one rainy night, riding a bicycle and wearing a scoutmaster's uniform; he said he wanted to become a Goon. He achieved his ambition – but in persona rather than person.

Milligan's contribution was not restricted to scripts and characters. A musician himself, he was responsible for bringing in Max Geldray (harmonica) and Louis Jordan soundalike Ray Ellington, whose interludes split the show into three sections. He also arranged the accompanying score with bandleader Wally Stott, and helped orchestrate the sound effects.

The *Goon Show* owed much to earlier styles of comedy. Its drumrolls and question-and-answer gags had a definite smack of music hall. There was, too, a cartoonish element: its name was partly inspired by the baddies, or 'goons', in the 1930s Popeye strip; and the way its characters were repeatedly destroyed then restored to life was, as Milligan admitted, very Tom and Jerry. But if it owed much, it gave more. Spike's alchemy transmuted these base materials into a philosopher's stone that affected anyone who touched it. From the Sixties onwards, the Goons' anarchic example permeated British comedy. Nor was its influence restricted to the British Isles: fugitive elements of Goonishness can be detected in US humour – the early work of Steve Martin and Dan Ackroyd, for example.

The *Goon Show* transformed comedy. It also transformed the life of its members. Sellers and Secombe used it as a launch pad to further stardom. Bentine never escaped from its shadow, being remembered less for his achievements as author and scriptwriter than as the legendary 'Fourth Goon'. And it drove Milligan mad. A moody perfectionist, who had suffered from manic depression ever since the war, Spike buckled under the pressure of creating up to thirty genuinely funny programmes a year. From the start he had shared the scriptwriting with others: usually Larry Stephens or Eric Sykes. As he became more depressed – eventually he would be hospitalised – Stephens and Sykes assumed a heavier burden. Occasionally they wrote whole episodes. But Milligan always

Overleaf: *The Goons in 1951: Peter Sellers, Harry Secombe, Spike Milligan and Michael Bentine*

returned to his typewriter, the angry not-so-young man of comedy.

The *Goon Show*'s cosy lunacy concealed a bitter sense of rebellion. 'It is against bureaucracy and for human beings,' Milligan announced. 'Its starting point is one man shouting gibberish in the face of authority, and proving by fabricated insanity that nothing could be as mad as what passes for ordinary living.' He hoarded newspaper clippings to prove his point. One of them mentioned Sir Rupert Shoobridge, who had arrived in Britain from Tasmania on official business only to find that a rat had eaten three of his suits, his top hat, dinner jacket and morning suit. He hastened to Savile Row, muttering, 'I would like to murder that rat'. Everything about the unfortunate Shoobridge – even his name – could have been taken from one of Spike's scripts. Art may have imitated life, but Spike's description of the show was really a description of himself. He was the man shouting gibberish, and the face in which he chose to shout it was that of the BBC. He nurtured a fearsome grudge against the Corporation, blaming it for his unremitting workload and for lack of experimentation. (When pressed for an example of the latter he cited, rather lamely, its inability to provide a sound effect of wolves howling.) He wrote his resentment into the scripts and later expressed it at every possible opportunity, preferably on prime time TV. Ironically, the organisation which Milligan hated was the one to which he clung. Whereas the other Goons worked simultaneously in TV and film, Milligan frightened producers with his intransigence. He refused even to write for other comedians. It would be two decades before he finally launched his own TV series. His single-mindedness, erratic health and tempestuous relationship with the BBC could have only one outcome. On 28 January 1961 the Goons broadcast their last episode. (The last, that is, until *The Last Goon Show of All* in May 1972.) In a typical blast, Milligan described his decade of creativity as the worst torture that could be devised for man.

The Goons were a living legend, their show a comedic comfort blanket so warm that members of the original audiences collected recordings just to hear their own laughter. It was hard to believe that they would not always be there. But, gradually, they weren't. Sellers (the youngest) died in 1980, Bentine in 1996 and Secombe six years later. Then Milligan went too. I remember 27 February 2002 vividly. It was a grey London morning and I was up top on a Number 9 Routemaster – the same type of bus that Bluebottle once caught from Finchley to America. ('But you can't catch a bus from Finchley to America.' 'I know. It only went as far as the Odeon and I had to walk the rest of the way.') A paper-stand had the headline: 'I told you I felt ill.' Everyone started to mutter. Even the tourists took notice. I wanted urgently to tell my children. Could Spike really be dead? I had grown up on the *Goon Show*. He was my childhood hero. Aged ten, I had sent off for, received, and subsequently lost, a signed photo. I had bought all his books. He had been a formative influence. For a moment I was in shock. Then I reassured myself that nothing had really happened. Bluebottle, Bloodnok, Grytpype-Thynne and all Spike's other characters were ageless. They would be waging their cardboard battles in silly accents for eternity. What were time or death to them? Bluebottle did not die every time he was deaded. And did Eccles wear a watch? No, of course he didn't; he had it written down on a piece of paper.

Joyce Grenfell
Janie Hampton

Joyce Grenfell was the best-loved female entertainer of her generation, perhaps of the twentieth century. Her gifts as a writer and performer of comic monologues have never been surpassed, and by the time she retired as an entertainer in 1973 her audiences on four continents had included such admirers as King George VI, Maurice Chevalier and Igor Stravinsky. Above all, she had the unusual gift of making her audience feel that she loved them as much as they loved her.

Joyce always claimed to be just a housewife who had walked on stage, but her childhood had prepared her for the limelight. Her mother was Virginian-born Nora Langhorne, the youngest sister of Nancy Astor MP, and they both taught Joyce to mimic any accent. Her father Paul Phipps, an architect, introduced her to the pleasure of observing people, especially on buses. Brought up in bohemian Chelsea, she went to smart private schools and was presented as a debutante at Court. A tall girl with huge feet, she was often the wallflower at society balls, but at nineteen she married Reggie Grenfell, a shy accountant.

As a young housewife living on the Astors' estate at Cliveden in the 1930s, she ran the local Women's Institute, wrote poetry for *Punch* and helped to entertain her aunt Nancy's guests. After one lunch, J L Garvin, the editor of the *Observer*, engaged her as the paper's first radio critic. This led to a meeting with the theatre impresario Herbert Farjeon, who asked her to perform a monologue she had written about the WI. Much to the fury of the professionals in his Little Revue, 'Useful and Acceptable Gifts' was an immediate success.

The Second World War brought more performing opportunities for Joyce. After a lunchtime concert at the National Gallery in 1942 she met Richard Addinsell, composer of the Warsaw Concerto. Together they wrote many successful sentimental ballads, including 'I'm Going to See You Today' and 'Turn Back the Clock', which aptly caught the public mood. In 1944 Joyce embarked with the pianist Viola Tunnard on two long ENSA tours across North Africa, the Middle East and India. For eleven months they performed three concerts a day, in Nissen huts and tented hospitals, to troops who were already familiar with her light, tuneful voice from the radio.

On leave in Cairo from this punishing schedule, she became the amorous target of Prince Aly Khan – a lover of race-horses, cards and women, and a deep disappointment to his father, the Aga Khan. Already married to the daughter of an English peer, Prince Aly wooed Joyce with dozens of red roses and dancing by moonlight. She probably managed to fend him off, but she felt guilty all her life for even feeling tempted. Infidelity and its repercussions became a theme of many of her monologues: the musician's wife in 'Life Story', for example, and the French lover in 'Dear François'.

Back in London, Joyce wrote new songs and sketches such as 'Oh! Mr du Maurier' and 'Travel Broadens the Mind', and joined Noël Coward in the first post-war revue, *Sigh No More*. 'Noël was an actor who wanted to be an aristocrat and Joyce was the opposite, an aristocrat who wanted to be an actor,' commented actress Judy Campbell. 'Both pulled it off rather well.'

In 1943 Joyce had tried straight acting, but soon realised that she could not act 'sideways' and, anyway, she preferred the audience to herself. Thereafter she only performed other people's material in films, such as *The Belles of St Trinian's* and *The Yellow Rolls-Royce*. Even then, directors had to accept that she would rewrite her part. 'This writer has obviously never met a real Duchess,' she proclaimed on the set of *The Million Pound Note*.

In the 1951 revue *Penny Plain*, for which Flanders and Swann wrote many of the songs, Joyce performed 'Joyful Noise' – a pastiche of a Handel oratorio composed by Donald Swann – as Miss Clissold, Miss Truss and Ivy Trembly from Wembley, who 'sometimes sing in **FFF** and sometimes *ppp*'.

After live theatre Joyce's favourite medium was radio. 'It's a one-to-one medium, and uses the imagination,' she said. In 1941 she wrote the first ever one-woman radio show, produced by Stephen Potter, the future author of *Gamesmanship*. Two years later they wrote and presented *How to Talk to Children* for the Home Service. Their astute social satire, mockery of contemporary etiquette and imaginative use of the medium pushed radio comedy forward by a decade. From this emerged the exasperated nursery school teacher, with Joyce's most memorable line, 'George, don't do that'. The *How* series ran for twelve years, using, among others, the voices of Celia Johnson and Roy Plomley. *In How to Listen (and How Not to)* Joyce was the first woman to speak on the Third Programme when it opened in 1946. She played nine different parts including 'Jean Gledding ATS of Bexley Heath' and a Mayfair flapper with a wireless-cum-cocktail cabinet fitted with a 'supersonic incessor switch and hypertonic two-way mega-cycle baffles'. Over the next thirty years Joyce wrote more radio material than any other woman in the twentieth century. She also secured the highest fees, rising from 8 guineas in 1939 to 250 guineas in 1963 for *The Billy Cotton Band Show*.

Fifteen years after she first went on stage, her first major solo show, *Joyce Grenfell Requests the Pleasure*, was launched in 1954, her songs and monologues backed by three dancers. After two provincial tours and a year in the West End it sold out for eight weeks on Broadway. In future shows, Joyce toured her shows with neither orchestra nor dancers, relying on the piano skills of William Blezard and the jewel-coloured costumes designed for her by Victor Stiebel.

Her success came from a combination of talent, observation and sheer hard work. She wrote over a hundred roles for herself, covering an enormous range: from the Scandinavian visitor at a cocktail party – 'I sink is so nice to say hello and goodbye quick, and to have little sings for eating is so gay'; to Shirley's cockney girlfriend talking about

A zest for living: Joyce Grenfell in one of her many roles

her boyfriend Norm – 'You know, the one that drives the lorry with the big ears.' Sometime she portrayed herself, as in 'Unsuitable', sung by a 'hat and gloves and pearls type' woman – 'I go jazzy when I hear the beat. I swing and sway in a groovy way.'

The role she most enjoyed (in 'Eng. Lit.') was the wife of an Oxbridge university vice-chancellor inspired by Sir Alec Douglas-Home's mother-in-law. A woman with strong values, she apologises for 'the regrettable absence of essential stationery in the visitor's closet'.

Joyce was able to laugh at people without malice, and her perfectly formed short stories contained a tiny but revealing slice of their lives. Each monologue took anything up to five years to write, yet lasted only two to eight minutes. It took her months of preparation before she could perform them as if she'd just wandered out from the kitchen and thought of an amusing anecdote. 'I do not improvise,' she said, 'but I do recreate the story every night.'

While 1960s humour was dominated by *Beyond the Fringe* and the atom bomb, Joyce's characters were still concerned with everyday problems such as finding the perfect picnic spot or disposing of a dead rabbit. The critics said Joyce was too domestic and apolitical, but her shows continued to sell out everywhere from Dover to San Francisco, from Glasgow to Sydney. When meeting fans in the street, however, she was always disappointed that they saw her as gawky games mistress Miss Gossage ('Call me Sausage') from *The Happiest Days of Your Life* rather than as an elegant actress.

Joyce's zest for living came from her faith in Christian Science. She talked often on the radio and in churches about her belief that goodness was all around and that if pain, evil and disease were ignored they would melt away. Apart from opening countless fetes and bazaars, she kept her enormous generosity secret. Young writers such as Clive James and Jeffrey and his brother Oliver Bernard received clothes, books and cheques. During the freezing winter of 1962 my widowed mother was taken to hospital, and Joyce arrived with steaming casseroles. She would put a pinny over her Chanel suit, whip a pair of Marigolds out of her crocodile handbag and whisk round the kitchen as she reminded us to do our homework. It wasn't until she sent us tickets to her solo show at the Haymarket that I discovered she had an evening job.

Her last live performance was at Windsor Castle for the Queen's Waterloo Dinner in 1973. Soon afterwards she lost her sight in one eye, but continued to appear on the BBC's *Face the Music* and give charity talks around the country. She died of cancer in November 1979, just a month before she would have been appointed a Dame of the British Empire. Over two thousand people attended her memorial service in Westminster Abbey, and many more waited outside.

Hancock's Half-Hour
Joseph Connolly

'Huur… Hancock's Half-Hour…'

Such was the modest and throwaway introduction – immediately recognisable and utterly memorable – breathed out resignedly by the Lad Himself. Just before that came the wonky tuba that ushered in every episode of what has now proved itself the longest lived and among the most loved and lauded television comedies of them all. So how could it be that Anthony Aloysius St John Hancock came to dominate British radio and television for more than a decade, only to die alone and in his forties as a result of the desperate cocktail of drink and despair?

I must have been about eight years old when I first saw a *Hancock* – which may or may not have been 'The Blood Donor', a legendary episode that has become almost a shorthand encapsulation of Hancock's whole career. I cannot have understood what this strutting and bombastic embodiment of self-righteousness in his shortie raincoat and Robin Hood hat was supposed to be or to represent – all I knew was that I was hooked immediately. It was impossible not to be fascinated by that big and half-melted pouchy hangdog face of his – his blankly amazed eyes, ever bulbous beneath the twin bristled doormats of his eyebrows. And every word that came out of him just seemed so… *funny*! Because of course (as is true of many TV viewers, even today) the thought of *writers* didn't enter my mind: all I saw was a man whose presence was unignorable – effortlessly trouncing the comments of others with the perfect *bon mot* or putdown, the instant retort and the eloquent protestation, all liberally spattered with muttered dry asides and those mimed innuendoes. But in common with all the great performers of his day, Hancock himself was very much aware of the supreme importance of his writers, and from very early on he was fortunate enough to be working with the best in the business: Ray Galton and Alan Simpson.

Hancock had been busy plying his radio persona since 1941, but his first real breakthrough came with *Educating Archie* – a perfectly extraordinary series for BBC radio, if only for the fact that its chief attraction was a ventriloquist, one Peter Brough. The eponymous Archie was – and we could only learn this from the odd grainy photo in the *Radio Times* – a stripe-blazered student made of painted wood and plaster, and Hancock was his tutor. Eric Sykes jointly scripted the series, a hit was born, and Hancock's name spread rapidly. He still guested on many other radio shows, however, and among all the writers of one-off sketches Galton and Simpson were fast emerging as favourites.

Hancock was always extremely serious about the quality of his work, his personal ambitions maybe unreasonably boundless. What he yearned for at this stage of his career was a whole show to himself, and very soon it was in the bag: the first episode of *Hancock's Half-Hour* – produced by the legendary Dennis Main Wilson and scripted by Galton and

Simpson – was aired on the Light Programme on 2 November 1954. Among the actors were, notably, he of the inimitable honk and whine, Kenneth Williams, and – even more notably – Johannesburg-born Sidney James. Galton and Simpson had both remembered his boiled-turnip features from the Ealing comedy *The Lavender Hill Mob* and thought him perfect as the perennial ducker and diver, forever on hand to rip Hancock off. The character of 'Sid' appeared throughout all the radio and television series barring the last – by which time Hancock very much resented his presence.

Hancock's Half-Hour extended to six radio series, ending in 1959: more than one hundred episodes (maybe half of which survive) of definitive and often very surreal humour – sound effects and the willingness of an eager audience to project their imaginations into the spirit of the dance making just about anything plausible. Only on radio could Hancock variously become – and only sometimes in his dreams – a sheikh, the driver of Stephenson's *Rocket*, a matador, a ballet dancer (!), a commando, a policeman, a test pilot… and even the prime minister. The start of the TV series, rather surprisingly, did not replace but was broadcast concurrently with the radio programmes – the first episode airing on 5 July 1956, just about halfway through the radio run.

It was with the instant and massive popularity of the TV show that the nation really came to know the man. Or did we? The star, after all, was called 'Hancock' (never Tony, and never any other name either) – but was 'Hancock' Hancock? Were we to believe that this failed and broke Shakespearean actor sharing digs with a cockney spiv at 23 Railway Cuttings, East Cheam – lugubrious and chirpy by turns, revolving on the spit of thwarted ambition, constantly strung between the parallel poles of trepidation and hope – was truly the Lad Himself? Was the black homburg and the astrakhan-collared coat – the supposed uniform of an impresario of the old school – an accurately drawn cocoon for the man within?

Well – yes and no. Galton and Simpson made a point of always working closely with Hancock – observing his mannerisms and traits, the way his face moved, matching the rise and fall of his voice against the cadence of the words, capitalising on this great gift of an actor they had before them. Hancock's face, indeed, became so utterly central to the performance that it is difficult to believe the character could work at all on radio (but he did, of course: superlatively. It was all in the peerless timing – a facility that Hancock now simply extended to each of his features in turn). It remains a tribute to the grasp and understanding of both Galton and Simpson and Hancock that their joint exploration of 'Hancock' never left room for the nationally famous and now very wealthy Hancock to get in the way. While both personae were keen to better themselves, Hancock, who yearned for international recognition – and his despair at never attaining it was partially responsible for his rapid decline – would forever be striving. 'Hancock', meanwhile, was busy longing for just a roof that didn't leak and maybe a stint of regular work. Whereas Hancock constantly drove himself towards the twin goals of stardom and perfection –

leaning ever more heavily on the bottle to blunt the edge of his frequent disappointment – 'Hancock' simply shrugged and threw in the towel: his occasional enthusiasms and enterprising schemes were eventually no match for his gullibility, obstinacy and loneliness – nor for his fatalism, the overriding conviction that he was *doomed* to fail (and with Sid around, it was always guaranteed).

The essential scaffolding of English comedy: pain, futility, embarrassment, hope, misguided faith and deep dissatisfaction, to say nothing of the inextricable tangle of snobbery, pretension and semi-education, were all to the fore in Galton and Simpson's writing and also, to an extent, within Hancock himself. But, like a stylish portrayal that is far subtler than caricature, all of this is writ large in the character of 'Hancock' (and, of course, played up for the sake of laughter).

By the time they reached the seventh and last TV series in mid-1961 – now called simply *Hancock* – Galton and Simpson were producing their very best work: Hancock's brilliant solo performance in 'The Bedsitter', the sideways take on *The Archers* entitled 'The Bowmans', 'The Radio Ham', 'The Lift' – and, of course, 'The Blood Donor'. Sid James – at Hancock's insistence – was conspicuously absent from this final series. He was making successful films by now, and this was the direction Hancock wanted too (for how else to secure the elusive international stardom he still craved?). But due to considerable strain in his creaky marriage, spasmodic though crushing self-doubt and an ever increasing dependency upon alcohol, Hancock was by now reliant on the teleprompt in practically every scene: his inability to learn lines was almost total. This, with hindsight, is maybe at its most apparent in, of all things, 'The Blood Donor'. In the early days each episode of *Hancock's Half-Hour* actually went out live, Hancock always putting in a superb performance first time. Even when they came to be prerecorded, the initial take was always the best. Now, though, the crucial fluidity of his movements (and of his features) was severely compromised by his having always to be in the sight line of the 'idiot boards'. None of this augured well for the world of films.

Galton and Simpson, however, rallied round with a screenplay. The result, *The Rebel* – a very funny satire on the contemporary art scene – was an instant success in Britain, though it signally failed to spread Hancock's name globally. And it is at this point, maybe, that a touch of paranoia crept in. Hancock became convinced that everyone else was holding him back – his lifelong agent Freddie (by now also his second wife, and with a drinking problem all of her own) and, crucially, Galton and Simpson themselves. He rejected their three ideas for a further film and they – having worked unpaid on the treatments for more than six months – retired to write again for the small screen, exploring and developing the Hancock–Sid relationship over many series of *Steptoe and Son*. Hancock went on to make a less than successful film called *The Punch and Judy Man*, appeared on several variety shows and, later, live on stage in Australia. By now, though, it had become horribly clear to everyone around him that he was a committed alcoholic almost out of control. A thirteen-part Australian television series was begun and three episodes filmed, but on 25 June 1968 Tony Hancock was found dead in his Sydney hotel room at the age of forty-four. He had swallowed a huge quantity of barbiturates, along with a bottle of vodka. He left a note that read: 'Things seemed to go wrong too many times.'

The lasting legacy, however, of thirty-seven extant television episodes of *Hancock's Half-Hour* out of sixty-three made (the others, unbelievably, were recorded over) will ensure forever that the light remains undimmed. This is even more remarkable in sight of the fact that none of the series – in stark contrast to so many other BBC stalwarts – ever seems to be repeated. They all simply replay in the memory – each of them a wonderful thing brought to us by two great writers and a superlative comedian with professional passion that burned in his heart, and whose eyes you were sometimes expecting to bleed.

Have I Got News for You
Suzi Godson

As host of the immensely popular comedy quiz *Have I Got News for You*, Angus Deayton
spent thirteen years biting the hand that fed him all his best material. But the bloodthirsty
tabloids had sweet revenge when his colourful private life became a front-page joke and
the BBC didn't find it funny at all. They fired him.

Have I Got News for You, which first appeared on our screens in 1990, was a studio-
based quiz show centred around the previous week's news, politics and current affairs. Not
exactly an original pitch, perhaps – Radio 4's *The News Quiz* was already in its thirteenth
year – but the programme was saved from the gameshow format scrapheap by the
ingenious casting of Angus Deayton as host. Previously best known for the 1980s radio
comedy *Radio Active* and its television offshoot *KYTV*, Deayton's astonishing ability to fill in
the blanks between team captains Ian Hislop (*Private Eye* editor and columnist) and the
comedian Paul Merton created some of the most acerbic and irreverent ad libbing ever
seen on telly. They were a particularly vicious trinity. Hislop adopted the role of cynical
smartarse, while Merton delivered a sort of deadpan surrealism. And in the middle,
Deayton, the urbane, sarcastic chairman, steered the show through libel and profanity,
barely raising an eyebrow.

Each week Hislop and Merton were joined by two celebrity guests, though as the
show matured the concept of two teams competing against each other became
increasingly irrelevant. Caption competitions, odd one out pictures, what happened next
clips and missing words games presented opportunities for razor-sharp humour, but there
was only ever one team – the three stars – and besides, Deayton made up the scores as he
went along. Merton's team usually won, though the prizes, like the guests, were merely a
foil for Deayton's gags: 'So, a copy of David Mellor's autobiography for the winners, a
copy of David Mellor for the losers…' Pretty soon even the dumbest guests realised that
they were just lambs to the slaughter, and generally those who were prepared to send
themselves up came out of it best. Veteran gameshow host Bob Monkhouse appeared on
the show twice, first in 1994 and again in 1997. Deayton introduced him by reminding
the audience that Monkhouse had once described comedy as being just like sex, then
added 'so expect him to be incredible for five minutes and then fall asleep for the rest of
the show'. Demonstrating perfect comic timing, Monkhouse was more than happy to be
the butt of his own jokes, saying that he 'once took marijuana but felt no effects, as he was
on coke at the time'. Guests who became defensive didn't fare so well. The legendary
episode with Paula Yates made the front page of several papers in 1995. Having left rock
saint Bob Geldof for INXS star Michael Hutchence, Yates was on the show as a PR plug
for her new book. Deayton described her as a woman who was 'famous for lying on a bed
flirting with celebrities, after which she would get up and go to work on *The Big Breakfast*'.

Hislop was particularly vitriolic throughout the show, not least about Yates' newly inflated mammaries, and eventually she broke under the onslaught. To her credit, in the midst of her histrionics she managed to retaliate to Hislop with one of the show's most famous quotes: 'Don't even look at me, you sperm of the devil!'

Few guests, though, generated as many gags as Neil and Christine Hamilton, who surprised everyone by agreeing to appear on the show in 1997. The former Conservative MP had recently been embroiled in a 'cash-for-questions' scandal and had lost his seat just the week before. Deayton introduced Hamilton and his wife uncharacteristically lamely by stating that they had brought the reputation of the Conservative party into serious disrepute by being happily married. Then Merton and Hislop went in for the kill. When Hamilton tried to sling some mud at the mudslingers, Deayton pointed out that it was 'much better to tell political jokes than to be one', and Hislop reminded viewers of a *Private Eye* cover featuring Hamilton saying it would take ten grand in a brown envelope to make him resign. Naturally, at the end of the show Deayton handed Hamilton a large brown envelope, telling him it contained his fees.

Though Deayton's critics claimed he was simply the highest paid autocue reader on the box, his effortless delivery belied a great deal of personal preparation. In 1997 when Michael Portillo lost his seat to Stephen Twigg, Deayton casually suggested that 'if you rearrange the letters that spell Michael Portillo, they come out as "I talk bollocks". Obviously that's give or take a letter.' During the last US election he uttered the following anecdote with a completely straight face: 'In the States, the election has become a so-called watercooler debate… [pause]… meaning that Americans gather round the watercooler at work and discuss whether it would make a better president than Bush or Gore.' And introducing Tracey Emin, Deayton described her as a contemporary artist who 'once exhibited a small tent covered in the names of everyone she had ever slept with, and is now working on a marquee for Peter Stringfellow'. Cue the laughter.

Having been given free rein and huge amounts of money to take the piss out of everyone onscreen, Deayton must have been aware of the risks he was taking offscreen. When the *News of the World* published an explosive kiss-and-tell, which gave a whole new meaning to the concept of 'current affairs', Deayton's private life suddenly became public property. The BBC halved his salary but allowed him to stay on, despite the fact that other presenters had been sacked for less. But trial by tabloid and the Governors of the BBC was nothing compared with what was to follow. Having graced the front pages for days, Deayton then had to go into the studio and face Hislop and Merton, knowing they would be ruthless (Merton had had the front page of the paper printed onto a T-shirt, which he revealed half way through the show). At the recording, free tickets were changing hands for more than £500, and seven and a half million viewers tuned in to see him take a roasting. It was rough from the start, but characteristically Deayton gave himself the first kicking by announcing that 'the loser of tonight's show is the presenter',

Unholy trinity: Ian Hislop, Angus Deayton and Paul Merton

and at one point he told viewers, 'don't adjust your sets, my face really is this red'. Then he introduced Christine Hamilton, who was reappearing on the show having recently reinvented herself in the jungle on *I'm a Celebrity: Get Me out of Here!* When Deayton made the mistake of describing her as the wife of disgraced former Tory MP Neil Hamilton she quickly retorted, 'Don't call my husband disgraced. If he's disgraced then what are you?' Clearly embarrassed, Deayton replied honestly, 'I don't know. Disgraced, I suppose'. Then he paused and under his breath added, 'But at least I didn't bang on about family values for seventeen years'.

Piers Morgan, editor of the *Daily Mirror*, said afterwards, 'When Christine Hamilton takes the moral high ground, you know the game's up'. When another spate of salacious allegations left BBC executives frothing at the mouth, Deayton's position was declared untenable. He retired as gracefully as he could under the circumstances, announcing that he would enjoy watching the show 'from behind the sofa'. At the first post-Deayton recording, in a tribute that was cut in the edit, Paul Merton summed up what many viewers were feeling at the time when he said that he would 'like to thank Angus for all his efforts in entertaining vast numbers of the general public over the years'. Then he paused for effect and added: 'How he found the energy to do this show as well, I'll never know.'

The Hitchhiker's Guide to the Galaxy
Michael Bywater

The Hitchhiker's Guide to the Galaxy became a cult shortly after its first incarnation on BBC Radio 4 in 1978, and remained a cult for far longer, and in far more different media, than anyone, including its author, ever imagined. It was, of course, a 'comedy great'. But between greatness and cult status there's quite a gulf. People have tried to codify it, but the rules don't work or all authors would write cults and get rich. So what *was* it about *Hitchhiker*?

It would be easy to point at the sci-fi element and blame it all on the nerfs, the dweebs and spods and anoraks, hungry for cult-following as a certain type of English spinster is consumed by a hunger for religion. Easy, but wrong. *Hitchhiker* only masqueraded as comedy science fiction; curiously, it was really nothing of the sort. Even more curiously, *Hitchhiker* left a legacy of… precisely nothing. There are no heirs, successors or assigns. More or less dud novels appear regularly with little puffs on the back saying the author is the new Evelyn Waugh, or the new Elmore Leonard, or, quite possibly, the new black. But none claim to be unveiling the new Douglas Adams, probably for two very good reasons. First, the people who might *like* to be the new Douglas Adams invariably misunderstand what he did; and, second, what he did was nothing new.

That's not to say that what he did was not splendid, or brilliant; just that, in form at least, Adams was no innovator. His comic and literary roots were in the world of P G Wodehouse and, beyond that, the ancient tradition of Everyman: the ordinary chap who finds himself unwittingly (and often witlessly) caught up in great events and who – crucially – remains unchanged. In a very basic sense – and this is rare in cult works – the *Hitchhiker* enterprise was without any moral dimension except, perhaps, for the principle that bewildered affability can be a useful tool for survival. Arthur Dent, the nice BBC chap swept away in the demolition of Earth, is no Pilgrim, and makes no Progress.

At the beginning of the radio series (and the book, and the computer game, and at least two versions of the film-which-will-probably-now-never-be-made) Arthur wakes up wanting only to get on with his day; but he has fallen foul of local council bureaucracy, which is about to demolish his house to make way for a bypass. But this is merely the faint, feeble echo of a further catastrophe, identical in form, immeasurably greater in extent: a giant fleet of spaceships, broadcasting the message: 'People of Earth, your attention, please' in perfect quadrophonic sound.

We all, of course, know what happens next. The Earth is to be destroyed to make way for a hyperspatial express route; Arthur Dent's friend Ford Prefect fills him up with beer (as a muscle relaxant) and peanuts (to make up for protein and salt loss) and propels them both aboard the first of many spaceships, where they find themselves in dreadful sleeping

Overleaf: *Simon Jones as Arthur Dent in the TV adaptation of* Hitchhiker

quarters, surrounded by grubby mattresses and other shabby impedimenta of alien life.

In this first section of the first part of this hydra-headed tale, Adams lays out more or less all the equipment – the instruments, the gadgets, the tools and gags and references – that he'll be using more or less constantly throughout the rest of his ludicrously short career. There are the echoes of heredity in the Council man Prosser's dreams of axes (he is, unknowingly, a direct descendant of Genghis Khan). There's the instinctive assumption of the medieval doctrine of correspondences – that great events in the Universe are mirrored in small events at home. There's the posture, if not the methodology, of the scientist that Adams sometimes fondly imagined he would have liked to have been.

And, of course, there's Arthur Dent, Everyman himself, the one to whom events simply happen, because of his own inertia, because he's been inadequately informed, or because that's just how he is and how things are. The only way he changes during his quest is by becoming wearier, warier and lowering his expectations: a very English progress. By the end of the five-volume trilogy (itself a literary gag that Wodehouse, whom Adams revered, would have loved), Arthur, facing the ultimate and irrevocable destruction not only of this universe, but of all possible universes, is as passive as he was at the beginning.

If the final destruction of all possible worlds reminds us fleetingly of Voltaire's attack on the optimism of Leibniz in *Candide* – 'all's for the best in the best of all possible worlds' – then we're on the right track. *Hitchhiker* isn't science fiction; it certainly isn't *comedy* science fiction. What it *is* is a satire on modern life, and a satire on satire itself. And unlike so much satire, it works, not by coming so close to the familiar that we can smell the sweat, watch the lice jump, see every open pore, but by creating an artificial distance so that the familiar appears, if only passingly, unfamiliar again. The technology, enchanting though it is – the Infinite Improbability Drive, the Babel Fish, the Total Perspective Vortex – is peripheral. So, too, is the mad inventiveness: the battle robot so angry at the unjust treatment of Marvin the Paranoid Android that it destroys the bridge on which it stands; the Bugblatter Beast of Traal, so stupid that it thinks if you can't see it, *it* can't see *you*; the Restaurant at the End of the Universe, reducing the final apocalypse to a Las Vegas-style dinner spectacular. What is *central* is the familiar seen anew. Adams took an Everyman and led him through the world – not just this world, but unimaginable worlds – and guess what? They all turned out to be the same.

And therein lies, I believe, the astonishing appeal of *Hitchhiker*. It is more akin to Ecclesiastes than to Asimov, Heinlein or Arthur C Clarke. Its message, in the end, is 'There is no new thing under the sun', whatever or wherever that sun may be. Technology changes nothing; it just makes it more so. People remain as foolish, as ambitious, as venal, as perplexed, as submissive and, in the case of Arthur Dent, as just plain *decent* as they always have been. Emotional maturity, if you will, consists in finally realising that, in one way or another, we are all in the same boat, whether that boat is a coracle or the *Heart of Gold* with its infuriating computer, Eddie, and its Infinite Improbability Drive.

That we should discover infinite loops of intertextuality in *Hitchhiker* should come as no surprise. Douglas Adams was steeped in literature (he read English at Cambridge) and, come to that, steeped in Englishness. He professed a delighted atheism, having discovered Darwinian evolution relatively late in his short life, but he betrayed his childhood chorister's latent

Anglicanism when he allowed the 'dying' Marvin to read God's last message to His creation: 'WE APOLOGISE FOR THE INCONVENIENCE.' Marvin's reaction is precisely what you would expect from an atheist finally given divine permission for his disbelief: 'I think,' he murmured, 'I feel good about it,' before 'the lights went out in his eyes for absolutely the very last time ever.' This note of melancholy, of perplexity and loss, persists throughout the entire *Hitchhiker* canon and is responsible for what I, at least, would argue is its greatness.

I said at the beginning it has spawned no legacy. Some have said that Terry Pratchett is Douglas Adams' successor, but, however splendid Pratchett's inventiveness may be, he lacks Adam's ludic imagination and his breadth of knowledge, and he is prone to fall occasionally into facetiousness. The odd, obsessional Adams fan-base is drenched in facetiousness; Adams himself, never. His tool of choice, instead, was the very English device of bathos; of which, of course, the most famous example was the Answer to the Great Question of Life, the Universe and Everything. Indeed, there are probably people around who believe that 'bathos' is Greek for 'forty-two'. Bathos, too, in the revelation that Arthur Dent's humankind was descended from the spurned detritus, shot into space – telephone sanitisers, PR men, hairdressers – of another, overcrowded civilisation. Bathos everywhere you look. Adams repeatedly plays the old find-the-lady trick, the nutshell routine, *tria iuncta in uno*: the world's pretty straightforward; no it's not, it's unimaginably complex; no it's not, it's pretty straightforward.

And that, perhaps, is why it's not only a cult but a cult which will survive. Unlike Aldous Huxley (who was appalled by his own inability to foresee the self-operated lift), Adams' technological inventions will not date. They are a trope: a device designed to point up our common humanity, our invariable tendency to get it wrong and to go *on* getting it wrong. We can build all the machines we like, and invest them with all the dodgy quasi-intelligence we can come up with, but *we* remain the same; that aspects of the world become more and more like an episode from *Hitchhiker* (call centres, predictive text messaging, recorded railway announcements which say 'I am very sorry for the delay' when there is no 'I' to be sorry) is a tribute, not to Adams' technological prescience (though Lord knows he was as big a techno-buff as you could find without moving into actual geekdom) but to his understanding of the immutability of human nature. Unlike mainstream SF, he is not dealing with the way we *might* live in an imagined future, but with the way we live now.

Douglas Adams once said to me, on the terrace of a restaurant called Le Provençal in Gordes, that he felt in some way, deep down, ill at ease in the world; that he sometimes thought that if he died everyone would be really rather relieved. It was the one thing that he was completely, utterly wrong about. Just as his grandfather announced on his retirement (putting his clock on the mantelpiece and taking to his bed, where he stayed five years until he died), Douglas, too, had 'done his bit'. To hope for, let alone to demand, more would have been foolish; as the posthumous *Salmon of Doubt* revealed, that particular well had run almost dry. He had moved on. Where he would have moved on to, had not the light in his forty-nine-year-old eyes gone out for absolutely the very last time ever on 11 May 2001, we can't tell. But the radio series, the books, the computer game, and, most of all, the *wit* lives on: a true comedy great, and much more besides.

Impressionists
Neil Wenborn

'And this is me.'

Never mind Watergate. Forget the disappearance of John Stonehouse. The mystery which most engaged the television-watching public in 1970s Britain was how a man capable of assuming the personae of so many of the great and good of his day – of adopting the inflections, the mannerisms, even the physical appearance of its politicians and entertainers, sports commentators, royalty – could imitate with such apparent ease the crooning of Frank Sinatra or Sammy Davis Junior, but seemed constitutionally incapable, however often he tested the patience of a loyal audience by practicing on their time, of holding a tune, or even a note, as himself.

The words which introduced the final number of the Mike Yarwood show – and under various titles and with the mysterious exception of 1970 there were Mike Yarwood shows every year from 1968 to 1987 – were the cue for families everywhere to hide their cringing in a nationwide flurry of clearing up the supper things and putting the kettle on. 'And this is me' must have been the Electricity Board's favourite catchphrase.

Mike Yarwood is the father of all impressionists. There were impersonators before him. Stanley Baxter was taking off Mae West and Harry Lauder when Yarwood was barely out of kindergarten. Peter Sellers could mimic anyone from Alec Guinness to George Formby. Peter Cook did a mean Macmillan. But when the history of the curious art of being other people comes to be written they will all be consigned to an introduction. The first chapter will be 'The Mike Yarwood Shows'.

Impersonation is living caricature. And caricature and satire have travelled together for centuries. Think of Gillray and Rowlandson, Steadman and Bell. But somehow Mike Yarwood managed to uncouple them. There was no edge to his impressions. There was none of Cook's barbed mockery. The kindly, self-deprecating man of John Humphrys' 1995 *On the Ropes* interview was too considerate of his subjects' feelings for that. He guyed his targets, not strafed them. Many he transformed, not with the bile-and-latex demonisation of *Spitting Image*, but rather into the acceptable face of themselves. And none more so than that grizzled political rottweiler Denis Healey, who became in Yarwood's hands a cuddly teddy-bear, defined not by punitive taxation policies or the humiliations of the IMF but by a pair of implausibly ramifying eyebrows. Even the most dispassionate of biographers, I suspect, will never quite succeed in separating the intellectual street-fighter of political reality from Yarwood's avuncular bumbler, forever chiding his opponents as 'silly billies'. Along with Edward Heath's seismic shoulders and Eddie Waring's 'up-'n'-under', Healey and his eyebrows have become a kind of latter-day

---

Old Labour: Mike Yarwood as Harold Wilson…

folk-memory, as entrenched in that parallel universe of the national consciousness as Canute's seaside hubris or Drake's game of bowls. Similarly, Harold Wilson's devaluation of sterling may be lost, along with flared jeans and Jason King's moustache, somewhere back beyond the blue mist of Thatcherism, but his 'pound in your pocket' is as real as Queen Victoria's 'We are not amused', despite the fact that neither of them actually said it.

Mike Yarwood had no agenda beyond entertainment – and entertain he did, (apart from that last song) superbly. His Christmas shows attracted enormous audiences, in their heyday knocking even those traditional Yuletide ratings champions, Morecambe and Wise, off the top of the tree. But watching them now is like looking into a different world, a place of escape – and not just from the harsh realities of the twenty-first century. For all their knockabout topicality they were an escape from the harsh realities of the 1970s and early '80s too. Where is Grunwick, you want to ask? Where are the Troubles? But that is to miss the point. It's like asking why Eric and Ernie never made jokes about Suez or the Cuban missile crisis. Yarwood was no alternative comedian in waiting. He was a product of the pub and club circuit, a one-man variety show. He was Dick Emery but with real-life characters.

It was Thatcher who did for Yarwood – and not only because Yarwood couldn't do Thatcher. That was part of the problem, certainly. Heath, Wilson, Callaghan were his stock-in-trade. They were, almost literally, second nature to him. But Thatcher was a different matter. To be precise, she was female. He had a go, but it was pantomime dame stuff and he knew it. For his last BBC series, *Mike Yarwood in Persons*, he conscripted Janet Brown who, with biology on her side, soon established a virtual monopoly on the Iron Lady, while Yarwood played to his strengths as her arch-inquisitor Sir Robin ('Mister') Day.

But for comedians of the old school, as Yarwood unashamedly remains, Thatcher threw down a weightier gauntlet than the challenge of fake breasts and a bouffant wig. Like Britain itself, comedy was changing, polarising. Thatcherism put the satire back in impressionism, and it did it with a vengeance. With the launch of *Spitting Image* in 1984, caricature reclaimed its roots. This was impersonation as savage as it was exact. No matter that the faces weren't human: the voices were real enough, as were the weaknesses they so mercilessly skewered. No one who saw the apocalyptic final sequence of the second 1984 series is likely to forget it: as the credits rolled over a collage of latex grotesques – Reagan, Chernenko, Botha, the Ayatollahs – Sting sang a specially rewritten version of the Police hit 'Every Breath You Take', in which the dark refrain 'I'll be watching you' seemed to find its predestined meaning. It was as chilling, as reassuring, a credo for satire as anything Pope or Juvenal could have devised. This polar climate was no place for Yarwood's breezier brand of impersonation, and by the end of 1987, his personal life unravelling into drink, his shows had gone the way of exchange controls and the British coal industry.

Behind the virulent puppetry of *Spitting Image* were the voices of the next generation of impressionists: Steve Nallon, Kate Robbins, Alistair McGowan – and a twenty-something wunderkind by the name of Rory Bremner, who by 1986 would be in front of the cameras

---

… and New Labour: Rory Bremner as Tony Blair

with his own first show. Other impressionists launched their careers from the springboard of Eighties satire. Phil Cool fused impressionism with Dada. Ronnie Ancona inherited the mantle of Janet Brown. The *Dead Ringers* team made their much-heralded transition from radio to telly. But it is Rory Bremner who defined impressionism as comprehensively for the 1990s and beyond as Mike Yarwood did for an earlier generation.

If Yarwood was Emery with real characters, Bremner is Yarwood with attitude. Not that he's a better impressionist. Who could surpass the almost frightening fluency with which Yarwood's face, his whole personality, would take on the lineaments of Hughie Green or Malcolm Muggeridge? But Yarwood's uncanny gift of mimicry was, you felt, always a fortuitous peg on which to hang his, or his team of writers', jokes. Bremner's is pressed into the service of a different cause. It never felt right to call Yarwood's targets 'victims'; you couldn't call Bremner's anything else. These are post-*Spitting Image* impressions – public warnings, a putting of the powers that be on notice that Bremner too, on our behalf, will be watching every move they make.

If this all sounds a little solemn, it isn't. Buttressed by the dialogues of his regular partners Johns Bird and Fortune, Bremner's relentlessly elided chains of stand-up take-off can be almost painfully funny. Nor does the *pro bono publico* extend to his wickedly only-just-over-the-top imitations of, for example, John Motson or Ainsley Harriott – celebs *du jour* who, when the Bremner archive is unearthed in thirty years' time, may stand in just as much need of footnoting as Yarwood's Larry Grayson or Magnus Pyke. There *is* a difference, though, and you know it as soon as you see it.

But does any of it *make* a difference? Perhaps. When, week after week in the dying months of 1990s Conservatism, Bremner's grey, strangulated John Major began his lonely address to the nation with the words 'I'm still here', you couldn't but feel it was bringing him that much closer to not being there at all. And just as the *Spitting Image* Steel or Kinnock bled indelibly into the real thing, so Bremner's righteous, all-things-to-all-people focus-groupie Blair – 'Amen… and of course our women, let's not forget' – hovers somewhere between caricature and a higher order of reality. Whenever the real Tony Blair says 'I say this to you', we hear Bremner's 'unto' instead. There's a kind of insidious public service here. You know it doesn't stop deviousness or corruption or war, but it nibbles at the foundations of our trust in what the powerful would have us believe, and it makes us that little bit more careful, if only subconsciously, to avoid exposing a similar flank ourselves. Like all satire, Bremner's impressions are darts aimed at hypocrisy and pomposity, and they stray beyond their targets. You feel them in your own flesh; you wince as you laugh. And if it wasn't for the laughter you wouldn't wince half so much.

It all seems a long way from Yarwood's affectionate, consensual twitting of the Establishment. But, after all, Mike Yarwood was about making people happy, an enterprise in which, at the top of his profession, he succeeded year after year with rollicking distinction. It was no part of his purpose to make anyone wince. It was just that, while by no means the only impressionist to do himself so much less convincingly than he did everybody else, he would insist on singing in the attempt.

I'm Sorry I Haven't a Clue
Sue Gaisford

In January 1992 Stephanie Slater, a young estate agent, was kidnapped and held prisoner in a coffin. After her release she told a newspaper: 'The constant sound of the radio was my greatest comfort… There was a comedy quiz with Willie Rushton, Tim Brooke-Taylor, Barry Cryer and Graeme Garden which made me laugh out loud. I thought to myself: Look at you, the situation you're in. And you're laughing!'

Ten years later, on a bright Sunday morning in the spring of the year 2002, three of those men stood in the booking-hall of a Tube station in North London. A small crowd had gathered, some of whom knew what was going on. The rest, sensing an occasion, were just hanging about in case anything interesting happened. Mysteriously, Nicholas Parsons was there and, even more curiously, Neil and Christine Hamilton. People with things to do glanced at them, pushed on through the turnstile and got away.

The occasion was the unveiling of one of those blue plaques which inform passing Londoners that upon this site once resided a venerable statesman, scientist or peer of the realm. Except that in this case the plaque was a memorial to an inimitable comic genius, the great Willie Rushton, who had died in 1996. The place was Mornington Crescent.

This otherwise unremarkable station has given its name to a game featured on that uniquely endearing and enduring radio show *I'm Sorry I Haven't a Clue*. As played by seasoned old hands, under the always capricious chairmanship of Humphrey Lyttleton, 'Mornington Crescent' has become the most arcane and recondite pastime in the history of broadcasting.

It's a game in which players take turns to mention London street names – but beyond that its workings are unfathomable. The rules are never explained, though the chairman occasionally requires the teams to observe, say, the Watling Street Variation or Morton's Second Parallel. To help new listeners who might well be confused, the team has published two useful guides. *The Little Book of Mornington Crescent* offers a comprehensive glossary and a brief history (the game was already, it seems, popular with the Romans). It also contains interesting recipes – for example, to make 'Coq Fosters' we should follow a good recipe for *coq au vin* but in place of wine use lager – and potted biographies of such legendary players as the precocious Mother Anna of Widdicombe (15?–16?). The real *aficionado* of the game, however, will prefer *Stovold's Mornington Crescent Almanac*, a valuable resource wherein are found such rarities as a short story by W Somerset Maughnington and an explanation of Rule 226 (Crabbit's Law) – as well as an alluring, if worrying, Personal Column.

It is strange that such elaborate attention should be paid to 'Mornington Crescent', which is, after all, just one of dozens of games belonging to a half-hour programme on Radio 4. Yet something about its impenetrable absurdity has entered the national psyche

– as Humphrey Lyttleton recently discovered. In real life he is, of course, a superb jazz trumpeter and, as such, was recently invited to take part in a Radiohead concert at Oxford. Although he knew that the members of the band were fans of the show, he felt a little apprehensive as he drove his old Volvo down the motorway, lest nobody in the young audience should know or care who he was. And then he realised that cars full of students were passing him, before slowing to lower their windows and call out in joyous recognition 'Mornington Crescent!'

Always defined as 'the antidote to panel games', *I'm Sorry I Haven't a Clue* was born in 1972, the brainchild of its most cerebral panellist, Graeme Garden. The idea was simply to get the right people together, give them a set of rules and hope that they'd be funny. It took a year or two to settle into its current form, but since the mid-Seventies it has never looked back. Jon Naismith, its current, longest-serving and most successful producer, decided to take the show out of the London studio and into theatres around the country: the recording sessions are invariably sell-outs. You'd be hard pressed to find a critic who hasn't reached for superlatives in its praise, and it has won innumerable awards, including two Sony golds. It has become simply the funniest programme on air.

Two and a half million people listen regularly each week, audience figures which many a television producer would envy. Indeed, it is occasionally suggested that it should transfer to television but, happily, this hasn't happened. It couldn't work. *Clue* is essentially an aural pleasure. For a start, there is Colin Sell. We don't need to see this much-maligned musician: it is enough to know that he is there, manfully accompanying people singing one song to the tune of another and enduring the chairman's scorn. 'Colin's piano playing is believed by faith-healers to possess miraculous powers,' says Humph. 'It once made a blind man deaf.'

Then there is the lovely Samantha, who travels with the team and keeps a tally of the points or, as the chairman puts it, 'scores everywhere we go'. This ethereal creature can seldom stay to the end of the show, usually having urgent philanthropic business to attend to. Her legendary – you might almost say mythic – voluptuousness is surely better imagined than glimpsed.

That could be true of all of them. Gorgeous as they undoubtedly are, we love them not so much for their physical beauty as for a far headier mix of qualities, including absurdity, intelligence, speed of repartee, inventiveness and geniality. They seem devoid of vanity or competitiveness, clearly relishing and developing each other's jokes. When Stephen Fry was appearing, the team was asked for new definitions. Fry defined the word 'cryogenics' as a tendency to look like Barry (Cryer) in photographs. Back came Barry, speed-king of repartee, defining 'stir-fry' as the arousal of Stephen.

Each week, Humph prepares the live audience for the sight of these mature gents by means of elaborately lurid introductions: in Leeds, for example, he extolled the city museums, speaking of 'curiosities of no financial value, relics of a bygone age, guaranteed

Graeme Garden, Willie Rushton, Barry Cryer, Humphrey Lyttleton and Tim Brooke-Taylor

to kill half an hour…' – a little emphasis on the word 'kill' followed by a tiny pause, then – 'Let's meet the teams.'

For the past decade the chairman's links have been written by Iain Pattinson, a past master of the baroque *double entendre*, who has written with and for the likes of Paul Merton, Ronnie Corbett, Graham Norton and Jack Dee. Sometimes the script is incomprehensible: 'As usual, it will be one point each or one away, otherwise it goes to the other side if not.' Sometimes it is abandoned with scant respect ('Who writes this rubbish?'). Sometimes Humph simply ad libs, as when he told Tim that his writing was so illegible that 'I have to pin it up on the wall and run past it'. Often what he says is riddled with innuendo. Such remarks look impossibly smutty in print: it takes a man of Humph's insuperable innocence to utter them and get away with it. He claims, with apparent earnestness, not to understand most of them, yet the man's timing is so impeccable that he could make a Tesco till-receipt sound funny.

The panellists' jokes are all their own. Naismith gives them a couple of days' notice of some of the rounds and leaves it in their hands, though he says that often the biggest laughs come straight off the cuff. Each has his own strengths: Tim is the garrulous motor, beloved of the audience; Barry remembers every joke in the history of the world; Graeme's laughs take – and last – longer than anyone's; Willie Rushton's were the most surreal. Asked to finish off a well-known saying beginning with the words 'Don't get your knickers in a…' Willie supplied the word 'boot-sale'. One of his contributions to 'Celebrity Misquotes' was: 'Rasputin: "Mine's a Babycham".' At the end of his last show, he and Tim sang 'Sisters' in the royal falsetto of the Queen and Princess Margaret. It's a large claim to make, but neither ever did anything funnier.

Since those days, many other comedians have partnered Tim. One of the best is Sandi Toksvig, who remarked, with provocative irony, that it was a privilege to follow such a distinguished line of women onto the show. Barry, predictably, picked up her challenge, assuming the reactionary character of the pub bore and explaining, in simple terms, how this clearly undesirable situation had come about: 'It all started in the War, you know. In the factories…'

Its elements of parody, punning and play make *Clue* a very Radio 4, very British comedy. It is hard to imagine any other nation enjoying, say, 'The Biscuit-makers' Film Club', featuring such gems as *The Singing Digestive*, *La Dolce Ryvita* and *The Penguin Has Landed*. Nor browsing through a hospital library for such masterpieces as *The Chronicles of Hernia*, *Lady Chatterley's Liver* or, indeed, anything with an appendix.

Perhaps it's an acquired taste, but it's worth the acquiring – for, as its addicts know, it brings comedy and laughter together like a horse and marriage. Besides, it's a sublime way to pass the brief interval of life before, as Humph is wont to say, the delicate mayfly of time collides with the speeding windscreen of fate, or the angry wasp of destiny flies up the trouser-leg of despair.

Monty Python's Flying Circus
Dick Vosburgh

A ragged, begrimed hermit emerges from the sea and struggles his exhausted way up the beach before falling in a spent heap and cueing the opening titles by croaking, 'It's…' Mozart introduces a television programme dedicated to recreating famous historical deaths. Unconvincingly simulated are the last moments of such 'evergreen bucket-kickers' as Genghis Khan, who gives a falsetto squawk, throwing himself in the air and landing on his back. Even less convincing is the death of Horatio Nelson, who is seen falling from a high window in a modern office block, screaming 'Kiss me, Hardy!' and landing on an offscreen pig. The squeals of more squashed pigs punctuate equally wild sketches; a television interview with a composer which founders because the host is more interested in his guest's nickname (Arthur 'Two Sheds' Jackson) than in his new symphony; a bicycle race pitting Picasso against Braque, Kandinsky, Mondrian, Chagall and others; a commercial in which four strident women fail to tell the difference between Whizzo Butter and a dead crab; and a night school where a language instructor is teaching basic Italian to a classroom full of Italians. I tell a lie – also in the class is a Teutonic type in lederhosen, but this error is rectified when he is sent off to the German class.

All of the above scenes appeared in the first edition to be screened of the pioneering, hilarious *Monty Python's Flying Circus*. The date was 5 October 1969. Not for nothing has BBC's Television Centre been called 'a hotbed of cold feet'; cautiously, they put out the début edition late on a Sunday evening, in a spot formerly reserved for the repeat of a religious discussion shown earlier that day. I must now declare a special interest: I worked with all the Pythons (except Terry Gilliam, who was then still in the USA) when we were fellow writers on the BBC's *The Frost Report* (1966). I later won sudden respect from my children when cast (as Van der Berg, a sinister, machine-gun-brandishing dentist-cum-spy) in the fourth *Python* show to be transmitted. That edition was subtitled 'Owl-stretching Time', one of the many titles originally mooted for the whole series; *Python* also could have been called 'The Year of the Stoat', 'A Horse, a Spoon and a Basin', 'Vaseline Review', 'Whither Canada?', 'Bunn, Wackett, Buzzard, Stubble and Boot', 'The Venus de Milo Panic Show', 'Sex and Violence', 'The Toad Elevating Moment', 'Arthur Megapode's Cheap Show' or 'Gwen Dibley's Flying Circus'. While in development, the series had been referred to in BBC quarters as 'Baron von Took's Flying Circus', as it was Barry Took, most astute of the Corporation's comedy advisors, who assembled its five Oxbridge writer-performers. Silly show titles came naturally to them: in a marquee at Oxford, Terry Jones and Michael Palin had appeared in a revue called *Loitering within Tent*, and John Cleese and Graham Chapman were in a Cambridge revue called *A Clump of Plinths*. At the same

Overleaf: *'And now for something completely different': the* Monty Python *team, 1978*

university, Eric Idle appeared in *A Girl Called Herbert*. It was Idle who recruited Minnesota's California-educated Terry Gilliam, provider of the surreal animations that gave *Python* its special look and freed its sketches from the tyranny of the final punchline.

The BBC found the new show's success as unexpected as the Spanish Inquisition. Apart from the *Daily Mail* and London's *Evening Standard*, the notices were wholly welcoming, and viewers were soon introduced to the unthinkable, mallet-wielding Arthur Ewing and his Musical Mice; the transvestite lumberjack; the man who complained about people who made complaints; the island solely inhabited by Alan Whickers; that invaluable firm 'Confuse-a-Cat Ltd'; the marriage guidance counsellor blatantly seducing the sexy Carol Cleveland, the show's resident non-drag woman; the 16-ton weight; Spiny Norman the giant hedgehog; Gilliam's knight in armour, who only appeared in order to hit someone over the head with a rubber chicken; Chapman's irate colonel, ever complaining about items being 'Silly!'; Jones' nude organist; Idle's leering virgin with his 'Nudge-nudge, wink-wink, say no more!'; Palin's equivocating pet shop proprietor; and Cleese's Ministry of Silly You-know-whats.

The show's third series boasted such manic classics as the cheeseless cheese shop, the 'All-England Summarise Proust Competition', Ken Russell's orgiastic take on *Gardening Club* and the interview with the man who claimed to have written anagram versions of every Shakespeare play – from *The Mating of the Wersh* to *Ring Kichard the Thrid*. (When the interviewer complained that 'Ring Kichard' was not an anagram but a spoonerism he was told to piss off.)

Despite these glories, however, one of the Pythons had grown restless. Cleese, who admits to having 'an extremely low boredom threshold', felt that too many of the team's earlier conceits were being recycled, and wanted to leave and explore other projects – among them a certain classic sitcom based on a tantrum-prone Torquay hotelier at whose hands he'd suffered while on a *Python* location in Devon. His dissatisfaction hardly surprised his teammates; near the end of the second series, Cleese, in the role of a doctor, had said of a weakish link, 'It's the end of the series – they must be running out of ideas'. Never was a line spoken with more conviction, yet John was persuaded to stay for a third series before departing. He would return, of course, to join the other five in the films *Monty Python and the Holy Grail*, *Monty Python's Life of Brian* and *Monty Python's The Meaning of Life*. *Brian* was their masterpiece, with the late, much missed Graham Chapman giving a charmingly vulnerable performance in the title role. In collaboration with Cleese, Graham had written such sketches as the Argument Clinic, the Piranha Brothers documentary, the dead parrot, the cheese shop, Arthur 'Two Sheds' Jackson, and the police interview with the manufacturer of the notorious chocolate assortment that included Crunchy Frog.

Although the fourth television series, tersely titled *Monty Python*, was Cleeseless, it teemed with vintage absurdities. I cherish the commentary on Epsom's Queen Victoria Handicap, a race in which, instead of horses, the runners were eight identically dressed Queen Victorias;

'*This parrot is no more*': *Michael Palin, John Cleese and a Norwegian Blue (deceased)*

the fight manager bursting with pride for his boxer ('The way he kept on fighting after his head came off!'); the appalling Garibaldi family of Droitwich, with Terry Gilliam in his finest role as the gross, bean-gorging Kevin; and Eric Idle's RAF officer whose wartime banter was so bizarre ('Bally Jerry pranged his kite right in the how's your father. Hairy blighter, dickie-birdied, feathered back on his Sammy, took a waspy, slipped over his Betty Harper's and caught his can in the Bertie') that even his fellow flyers were baffled.

After six weeks, it was all over. That gigantic bare foot, accompanied by the martial strains of Sousa's *Liberty Bell*, had made its final flatulent descent.

Morecambe and Wise
Christopher Dunkley

On 25 December 1977 Queen Elizabeth II and her family delayed dinner until they had finished watching the *Morecambe and Wise Show*, which included the '*South Pacific*' number with solemn middle-aged BBC journalists such as Frank Bough and Richard Baker dressed as American sailors apparently performing amazing feats of gymnastics. During the late 1960s and early Seventies it had become a habit with the royal family to delay dinner until after the show, as it had with so many others across the land, from market-stall traders to Hampstead intellectuals.

That year the Christmas show on BBC television attracted 28.8 million viewers, more than half the population of the UK. No comedian or comedy duo had achieved such a thing before; indeed few programmes of any description, apart from royal weddings, had ever come anywhere near such a figure, nor – given the proliferation of television channels and the fragmentation of audiences in the twenty-first century – does it seem likely that anyone will ever do so again.

There was no single obvious thing which set Eric Morecambe and Ernie Wise apart from their contemporaries. Like many comedians, they came from the North of England and began their careers very young. Eric, whose real name was Bartholomew, changed it to Morecambe because that was where he was born. To follow suit, Ernie almost changed his to Leeds, but in the end simply cut Wiseman back to Wise. Ernie, born in November 1925, the elder by six months, learned to tap dance in his mother's kitchen when only six and by the following year was earning money in working men's clubs doing three gigs a week in a double act with his father.

 For the rest of his life Ernie would remain, at heart, a song and dance man. He would also remain, as from the start, concerned with just how much he was paid and how much was stacking up in the bank – one of the many genuine characteristics which would later emerge repeatedly in the double act. From the very beginning Eric was the comedian, though he too learned to sing and dance. Working as they did on the variety circuit in the 1940s, it would have been almost impossible not to. At that time the variety theatres such as the Liverpool Empire, where Morecambe and Wise first appeared as a double act in 1941, were either former music halls or indistinguishable from them in spirit.

So although they worked from a remarkably early age on radio, getting their first break there from the BBC in the middle of World War Two in 1943, Morecambe and Wise were members of the last generation of comedians to learn their business within the traditions of the music hall. They shared this experience with others who became

---

'Bring me sunshine': Ernie Wise and Eric Morecambe in 1976

successful, including Tommy Cooper (whom Morecambe once told me he admired above all), Ken Dodd, Max Miller, Eric Sykes and Norman Wisdom. The break occurred between that group and the next generation, Peter Cook and Dudley Moore, John Cleese and the Pythons, and their successors Rik Mayall, Eddie Izzard and so on, whose experience was gained entirely after the death of music hall and the variety theatres.

If there is a single factor that explains the unique popularity of the sixty-nine Morecambe and Wise shows made for the BBC between 1968 and 1977, perhaps it is the hard graft of the 1940s and '50s when 'the boys' had to work to please live audiences in variety theatres. However, if that really was the answer then you would expect that the programmes they made for ITV would be as good as those they made for the BBC. Yet although their first ITV period, from 1961 to 1967, was impressive, it was the BBC shows which were the true classics, and the final batch made with ITV between 1978 and 1983 was sadly inferior.

As so often in such matters, it is hard to avoid the conclusion that it was a fortunate combination of factors which produced unique results. Bill Cotton Junior, better than anyone in British broadcasting at that time at nurturing talented entertainers, brought Morecambe and Wise into the BBC and cosseted them after Lew Grade at ITV refused to raise their fees to what they thought they deserved. Cotton asked John Ammonds to produce the shows and Cotton gives Ammonds credit for being almost a third member of the act. It was Ammonds who first thought of seeking guest appearances from people as eminent and serious as Robin Day and as popular as Cliff Richard, and Ammonds who introduced the closing dance after spotting Groucho Marx doing it in *Horse Feathers*.

Above all it was the BBC's appointment of Eddie Braben as chief scriptwriter which raised the shows to a new level. Instead of simply writing gags to suit their talents, Braben observed the relationship between Eric and Ernie in real life and wrote sketches which reflected that reality. It takes a peculiarly powerful example of what Coleridge called 'that willing suspension of disbelief' in the onlooker to accept – blithely and without a moment's doubt – that the two male comedians naturally and habitually, not to say entirely asexually, occupied the same double bed. Thanks to Braben's scripts, such seemingly surrealistic touches were universally accepted without a murmur.

Ask precisely how Morecambe and Wise differed from so many other comedy acts of that or any other period and the answer is that the audience did not just like them or laugh with them – millions of British viewers loved them. So did fellow performers. By the end of their BBC stint it seemed that there was not an actor, singer or celebrity of any description who would not appear with them. Most would have given their right arms to do so.

Glenda Jackson, at that time a desperately serious actress who was making her name with the Royal Shakespeare Company and in formidable roles in the Theatre of Cruelty, declared in a 1994 documentary that it was her guest appearance on the *Morecambe and Wise Show* as Cleopatra in one of Ernie's plays ('All men are fools and what makes them so is having beauty like what I have got') which brought her the lead in the Hollywood comedy *A Touch of Class* and thus won her an Oscar. Jackson, who appeared not once but five times as a guest on their show, said of Morecambe and Wise: 'The incredible thing about them was not only that they were admired – I certainly admired them – but that they were loved by their audience. I don't think that's too extreme a word. And that's what made it so easy to say yes to their requests to appear on the show. The response their audience had towards you was such that you as a guest star were enveloped in that love as well.'

That highlights one of the brilliant aspects of the great Morecambe and Wise shows: that although it always seemed as though the guests were being sent up rotten by the comedians, what was actually happening was that their reputations were being enhanced. When Shirley Bassey, in a glittering evening dress, lost her right shoe as she descended the staircase singing 'Smoke Gets in Your Eyes', Eric slithered on at her feet with a replacement – substituting an army boot for the spangled pump. Later he managed to get her left foot into the matching clodhopper so that the shapely torch singer had to stomp off in a huge pair of black leather boots. It looked like ridicule, but of course everyone loved her for being such a sport.

The conductor André Previn had his dignity similarly assaulted, first being welcomed as 'Andrew Preview', then being subjected to Eric's ludicrous chopsticks rendering of 'Grieg's piano concerto, by Grieg'. Complaining that Eric is playing all the wrong notes, Previn is grabbed by the lapels and told by the smug comedian, 'I'm playing all the *right* notes… but not necessarily in the right order, I'll give you that, Sunshine'. It seems clear from remarks made subsequently, not just by Jackson but by many guests from Previn to newsreader Angela Rippon – whose legs suddenly became her most famous attribute after she displayed them in a Morecambe and Wise dance number – that what they valued as much as anything was the unique sense of affection bestowed by the audience upon those appearing in the show.

Watching the Previn sketch today can still make you laugh, even if you have seen it a dozen times, but the most striking moment occurs after all the big gags have been done and Previn sits down at the piano and plays the opening bars of the concerto properly. Morecambe and Wise, offended at being shown up, head sulkily for the wings until Previn capitulates and reverts to Eric's honky-tonk version. 'That's it! That's it!' the boys cry, scampering back to the piano, where they go into a soft shoe shuffle to accompany the maestro's travesty. They beam, Previn grins, and on the dais in the background the members of Previn's orchestra, probably believing they are out of shot, laugh so hard they nearly fall off their chairs. The atmosphere is one of universal good humour and deep affection.

That, surely, is what the royal family valued, what the national audience loved, what took Morecambe and Wise to that unequalled rating of 28.8 million, what still shines out from their recordings today, and what will continue to be unmistakeable to any sympathetic viewer for generations to come.

The Office
Stephen Moss

I missed the first episode of *The Office* – and I wasn't alone. It was shown in a far-from-primetime slot on BBC2 in July 2001 to an audience of one and a half million, presumably devotees of co-creator Ricky Gervais' previous hit-and-miss comic outings in *The 11 O'Clock Show* and *Meet Ricky Gervais*, or perhaps viewers who took the mock-documentary format seriously and thought the programme was a management primer. Either way, the audience was small, the pre-publicity limited, and the scheduling – the start of the summer holiday period – did not suggest overwhelming confidence in this everyday story of life in a Slough paper merchants.

Not catching those early episodes may have been a godsend, because the responses of some of those who did now read like those wonderful notices by Viennese critics who dismissed Beethoven's Choral Symphony as long-winded. 'How this dross ever got beyond the pilot stage is a mystery,' complained Victor Lewis-Smith in the London *Evening Standard*. 'The series would be very funny if David Brent were not quite such a horrible monster… One can scarcely wait another four weeks to see him sacked,' said Peter Paterson in the *Daily Mail*. 'Goodness knows how it will manage to sustain another five episodes,' added Jaci Stephen in the *Mail on Sunday*. It would be interesting to know if they attended all those black-tie dinners a year later at which Gervais and co-writer Stephen Merchant were showered with awards.

The first time I saw *The Office* was on a plane – on one of those tiny, fuzzy, back-of-the-seat screens – and for some reason I watched it without headphones. Even in those constrained circumstances I knew it was good. It was the episode set in Chasers, one of Slough's most fashionable nightspots. Even as a strobe-lit mime, Gareth's sad, sunken face and the body language of the principals – the slobbish, drunken Brent, the predatory Chris Finch, Tim in his beige mac – made it fascinating. I was added to the list of those who wanted to know more; the cult was growing.

David Brent – the bombastic but desperately insecure boss of the Slough branch of Wernham Hogg – is now a legendary character, comparable to Captain Mainwaring and Basil Fawlty in the pantheon of comic creations. The three share a common bumptiousness that invariably ends in disaster, but none is wholly unsympathetic: they are archetypal Brits doing their best; self-appointed organisers profoundly unsuited to their jobs. Brent could no more run an efficient office than Fawlty could keep a decent hotel or Mainwaring repulse the German army. They are hard-pounding failures who can't see that their own defects are the source of their disasters. As with all great comedy, they are essentially tragic figures.

The boss: co-writer Ricky Gervais as David Brent in The Office

Brent is not the monster that Peter Paterson perceived. When he reads John Betjeman's poem 'Slough' ('Come, friendly bombs, and fall on Slough / It isn't fit for humans now') in order to attack the sentiments (or lack of them) of the poet, one applauds his humanism. Most of his staff are, indeed, leading lives of quiet desperation and he wants to make them better, but his fatal lack of self-knowledge defeats him at every turn. All his attempts to be a caring boss – his self-proclaimed distaste for sexism and racism, his championing of the rights of the disabled – end up undermining those he wants to defend. He is part of the problem, not part of the solution.

Brent is weak, selfish and stupid, but not monstrous. When he is eventually sacked, we feel not glad, but sad. His tears seem real: his job, this wretched office, is his life. He is so much nicer and more human than his effortlessly successful rival, Neil. Brent needs this job, the security of this family, and we know that without it he would collapse.

Gervais was once asked what his TV alter ego would do at Christmas. 'He'd spend it with his sister, though her kids hate him staying there,' he replied. 'She lives in the Didcot area.' I believe this – and I believe that Gervais believes it. Everyone in *The Office* is fully formed – when I did eventually catch up with that first episode I understood and empathised with these people within ten minutes. There is no canned laughter in *The Office*, and there are no canned characters either. The eleven episodes – Gervais has said there will not be another series – are more a five-and-a-half-hour minimalist drama than a sitcom. The silences resound; the emptiness fills the screen. This comedy is akin to Pinter's, occupying that no man's land sometimes called life.

Brent is the central character in the early episodes, but in the second series his antics become more absurd, the comedy coarser, the embarrassments less subtle; we are no longer laughing but squirming and seeking refuge behind the sofa. By now our attention, when we have returned to the armchair, has shifted elsewhere – above all to Tim's relationship with Dawn. This is brilliantly done: the way they flirt, play with each other's hair, gently touch each other's arms. We are certain that Dawn will leave the likeable but philistine Lee (blue-collar, likes Florida, anticipates a lifetime of children and drudgery for his wife-to-be) for the sensitive Tim. Tim and Dawn are the perfect couple; this dream must come true. But it doesn't: in a superb scene played out in a small room behind glass so that we can hear nothing of what is said, Dawn ultimately rejects him. The degree to which I cared that Tim and Dawn should end up together confirmed to me that this was a 'comedy' like no other I had ever seen.

Presumably, some work does get done at Wernham Hogg, but it is never clear how or when. In that it resembles all offices. Occasionally, the staff take a call or send an email, but mostly they are arguing, playing practical jokes on each other or trying to get a colleague into bed. They worry about losing their jobs, but it is never clear what jobs they have to lose.

Most of the men in *The Office* are weak dreamers. Brent is forever harking back to his failed music career (here, as elsewhere, Brent's CV mirrors that of Gervais, who released two singles with a band called Seona Dancing that just about made the top 200). Gareth is obsessed by the army – he had a brief stay in the Territorials – and spends most of his time fantasising about killing the enemy with his bare hands. Tim wants Dawn; Chris Finch wants sex and lager (though probably not in that order); the mountainous Keith appears to have accepted that his life is destined to be unremittingly tedious, though he comes briefly alive when he DJs an office party (pop music as healer and energiser is a recurrent theme). The women are far stronger and hold all the cards. Donna's sexual frankness is endlessly embarrassing to the seedy Brent and emotionally immature Gareth – men who are constantly alluding to sex but, like the blazered man in the *Monty Python* sketch, never actually try it out. Dawn has the strength to make the break with Tim. Jennifer Taylor-Clark, Brent's no-nonsense, mini-skirted boss from head office, is a terrifyingly driven career woman; no idle dreams for her, she intends to win for real. The sexual politics are as vivid and perfectly realised as everything else at Wernham Hogg.

Perhaps it's not surprising that some of the early critics took against *The Office*. It wears the trappings of a docusoap but is of course a spoof; it purports to be a comedy but sometimes you want to cry; by the end it has become a full-blown drama. It defies every genre, and it is to the eternal credit of the viewing public that they found it and turned it into a word-of-mouth success. I and all the others who jumped on to the bandwagon later – via repeat showings on TV, video and DVD release, or even bizarre encounters at 35,000 feet – can claim no such credit. If you saw that first episode back in July 2001 and got it straightaway, your taste is impeccable. It is far easier to recognise genius when you have been told where to look.

I hope Gervais is true to his word and doesn't make another series (he hasn't ruled out one-off specials, though even these might be otiose). Follow the example of Cleese and don't damage your creation. A bad sitcom is endlessly extendable: it is just as bad at the end as it was at the beginning. *The Office* – with its precisely painted characters and surreal yet entirely logical, tautly written dialogue – is a perfectly realised world. It has the economy, precision and satisfying completeness of a good novel. The horse is alive, so don't start flogging it.

We can, I think, have some confidence in Gervais. 'I've done enough things when I've thought, "I wish I could give the money back, that was shit",' he told one interviewer. 'It's better to just keep saying no.' Let the eleven episodes be endlessly replayed, like *Dad's Army* and *Fawlty Towers*: testament to their quality; an ambiguous *hommage* to Slough; a fascinating portrait of the surrogate family office life provides; and a warning never to go to Chasers on a Wednesday night.

Only Fools and Horses
Shyama Perera

I grew up on a council estate near the Edgware Road flyover. I don't remember anyone around Hall Place driving a Robin Reliant, but we were north of the river, which is a few degrees closer to the sun than the estate in Peckham, Sarf London, where Derek and Rodney Trotter, otherwise known as Delboy and the Little Plonker, were being raised within, and to, the great heights of Nelson Mandela House. 'We're fifteen minutes from the West End, and fifteen minutes from London,' Rodney once commented. 'Yes,' said his Uncle Albert. 'And fifteen minutes from the ground.'

Fifteen minutes from the ground was the flat that, week on week, became a running gag in its own right as increasingly bizarre job lots – Russian videos, boxes of tomatoes, pre-blessed communion wine (white, unfortunately), portable computers ('It's got RAM, it's got ROM, it's got them red and green lights: everything') and buzzing mobiles – took up precious floor space.

It was, of course, the home of Trotters Independent Trading, or TIT plc: a business that was distinguished by its ability to throughput anything and everything that was saleable, and quite a lot that wasn't.

I still remember the classic night that Del, on an adrenaline high, brought home a consignment of knocked-off dolls: 'They're Barbies or Sindys.' In fact, they were inflatable sex dolls. Left against a radiator, two were activated by dodgy inbuilt propane gas cylinders and popped up suddenly, fully blown, from behind the Trotters' padded Seventies cocktail bar…

And the cocktails: the pina coladas and the daiquiris, the umbrellas, the plastic monkey twizzle-sticks, the pieces of fruit. It was a sad day when Del temporarily became a yuppie, holding his Filofax before him like a crucifix, and turned to drinking red wine spitzers (sic). He was convinced it improved his chances with the girls, but as he went to lean nonchalantly against the bar at the upmarket watering hole he'd taken to frequenting, he only discovered as he disappeared from view and described a perfect arc to the floor that the counter had been raised for access. There are many comedy moments that can match it, but few surpass it.

Perhaps that's because, at the heart of the drama, was the perfect double act, with Delboy playing Morecambe to Rodney Trotter's Wise. Alexander Smith once said: 'A man gazing at the stars is proverbially at the mercy of the puddles in the road.' Del was always in a puddle somewhere, dragging Rodders after him, keeping his younger brother in line with a verbal slap: 'Come off it, Rodney, you couldn't sell a black cat to a witch.'

In Derek Trotter, David Jason gave us a character who was both charming and

'This time next year we'll be millionaires': Rodney, Delboy, Granddad and (overleaf) Uncle Albert

cunning. A man who started off the series small, slim and dark, and emerged after seven seasons round, middle-aged and grey. His changing look was part of the humour. Put on a healthy eating plan for abusing his system, Del pushes away a bowl of muesli: 'It looks like something that's been swept out of a pigeon loft.'

But it was the relationship between the leads that made the show. Left to raise his brother after the early death of their mother and the disappearance of their father, Del exercised both patriarchal power and tenderness towards the younger man. Rodney's resentful upward dependency often added poignancy to the comedy. 'All the things we have ever had in life,' Del says at one point, 'have come from my intelligence and my foresight.' 'Well, I'm glad somebody has owned up,' says Rodney, sourly.

When Rodney marries the posh Cassandra ('Who's that tart?') Del withholds a large payment to violent gangsters so he can finance the deposit on his brother's marital home. It is truly moving TV when Rodney, shitfaced after his stag night, stripped to his boxer shorts with a giant L-plate pinned to the front, rails at Del for keeping the money from him. It is on the table: and Del, hiding in the bedroom, is nursing the aftermath of a severe beating from his debtors.

At the wedding, as Rodney leaves, the profound loss on both their faces says it all. Indeed, as in real life, the quickfire dialogue in *Only Fools and Horses* often belies true emotions, which are there in the facial expressions. Some characters are virtually mute: when Del eventually falls in love with Raquel Turner, the actress turned stripper, there are whole episodes where she hardly says anything.

This is all down, of course, to the brilliance of the writer, John Sullivan, who created a huge cast of regulars, all of whom stand on their own. Uncle Albert, with his Ancient Mariner looks, all-purpose war stories and turkey neck was, after the death of Granddad from the earlier series, the perfect foil to Del's cocky confidence and Rodney's inbuilt pessimism. 'My granddad lived to eighty-one,' Del says in one episode. 'That's a good age.' 'It weren't for him,' Albert replies drily. 'He died.'

Later there's a moving scene where Albert runs away to Tobacco Road, his childhood home, to discover it's been yuppified into millionaire flats. 'There used to be streets around here… lots of two-up-two-down houses: dockers' mansions we used to call them… ragamuffins kicking footballs up against the wall… They were rough people, but they were good people. Look at what they done to it now.' 'Yeah,' says Del, admiring the view. 'It's terrific, innit?'

The male household was augmented by a male social life that wives and girlfriends could affect but never alter. Always at the bar in The Nag's Head was Trigger the roadsweeper, who lived in a parallel universe where Rodney was called 'Dave'. In the last series, as we await the birth of Del's baby, he tells the publican: 'If it's a girl they'll call her Sigourney after the actress. And if it's a boy, they're naming it Rodney: after Dave.' Perhaps you have to see it to understand, but it still cracks me up.

As indeed does the thought of Boycie, the smarmy local car dealer, with his camel coat and ever-present cigar, married to the 'Peckham bike', Marlene, with her Joan Collins wardrobe: 'Yes, I noticed you approach my wife and shake her warmly by the 'arris.'

Perhaps it touches a chord because I knew blokes just like that. They weren't just my neighbours but my colleagues too. At that time, the beginning of the 1980s, I was crime reporter on a local rag in Stratford. I remember one day writing up a robbery where a delivery driver was tied to a tree in Epping Forest and his cargo of portable colour TVs taken. As I typed, our sports desk boys were busy flogging them off. It was normal to be sitting in the pub when someone would walk off the street with a roll of dodgy jewellery, offering belcher chains and nine-bar-gate bracelets for half the retail price.

It's part and parcel of being in a community where you duck and dive to make a buck – or to quote the *Only Fools and Horses* theme tune, also by John Sullivan: 'Stick a pony in my pocket / I'll fetch the suitcase from the van / 'Cos if you want the best 'uns / But you don't ask questions / Then, brother, I'm your man…'

Through his characters, Sullivan has introduced some classic phrases to the vernacular: plonker, dipstick, lubberly jubberly, no way Pedro, this time next year we'll be millionaires… Only Del, with his rolling confidence, could turn *'petit déjeuneur'* and *'cordon bleu'* into exclamations.

Since the last series more than ten years ago there has been a regular Christmas special, but the only one of those I saw had Del and Raquel breaking up for a large part of it, and I found it difficult to watch – because I had grown up, and continued to grow up, alongside them. There were too many parallels, as getting older and the pressures of real life started to encroach on the humour of the residents of Nelson Mandela House.

Only Fools and Horses, for me, encompassed all that was funny and raw about social transition in Britain in the 1980s. Del Trotter was the archetypal new man: the clever but uneducated cardsharp who had the wits and the ambition to make something of himself and could, in Thatcher's new Britain of deregulation, claw his way up the ladder. He personified the man who has no choice in life but to keep moving in order to survive, and he did that with the humour, the wit, the nerve and the generosity of any half-decent council-house boy.

That was what was magic about the series. However ludicrous some of the scenarios, the premise on which they were built was a baseline I, and millions of others, recognised. I still get pleasure from watching the re-runs: the situations themselves have dated, but the one-liners are still so clever: 'I'm going to take you out onto the balcony to see if the EEC has changed the laws on gravity…' Lovely.

Long live Hooky Street.

Pete and Dud
Mark Lewisohn

The four university graduates didn't know one another, didn't believe their work together would last very long and had little affection for the title given to their show. Yet the unheralded Edinburgh Festival revue *Beyond the Fringe*, staged in the first year of the Sixties, changed the course of comedy and altered their lives irrevocably. Alan Bennett, Peter Cook, Jonathan Miller and Dudley Moore's new style of revue – comedy with intelligent subjects, groundbreaking in its pointed topicality and outspokenness – created an explosion of 'satire' (Fleet Street's label of convenience) which rumbled throughout the decade.

When, by 1964, the quartet finally bowed out, they exited through separate doors, never to work together again. Miller, a qualified doctor, went into stage direction; Bennett, the history don, became a playwright and novelist; Moore, the organ scholar, resumed composing film scores and ballets and, as a brilliant pianist, fronted a modern jazz trio; Cook, the linchpin of the entire venture, the revue writer, Establishment Club owner and *Private Eye* benefactor, drifted into bits of performance and writing, bedazzling with everything he touched.

And that appeared to be that, until a few months later when Cook and Moore struck up a partnership. It happened unplanned, when producer Joe McGrath offered Moore his own series on the BBC's newly launched second channel. Moore wanted to bring in Cook. In the latter part of their period in *Beyond the Fringe* Cook had introduced some new two-hander sketches. All were brilliant, especially 'One Leg Too Few'. In this, Dudley, hopping around as a one-legged man named Mr Spiggott, comes to visit Peter, an agent conducting auditions for the role of Tarzan. Peter – 'I couldn't help noticing, almost at once …' – attempts, with admirable English reserve, to let him down gently. Spiggott, remarked Cook calmly, was a 'unidexter'. It was a work of genius and would become the pair's greatest hit, performed time and again in later years. So Moore asked Cook to join him in his BBC2 show, instantly reclassifying his solo endeavour as a joint venture. Success was immediate, cementing a double act that ran for almost fifteen years and invokes, still, a sense of deep, unadulterated joy.

The show was called *Not Only... But Also*, and it hit the ground running. In one opening-edition sketch Moore conducted an interview with Cook's Sir Arthur Streeb-Greebling wherein the aristocratic numbskull discussed his life's work: teaching ravens to fly underwater. In another, John Lennon – he and Cook were friends – helped Moore and comic actor Norman Rossington spoof the BBC's arts documentary *Monitor*. And in a seven-minute piece informally titled 'Sex Fantasies', Cook and Moore turned television comedy on its head with an original and breathtakingly funny sketch featuring two scruffy ignoramuses named Pete and Dud. Pete, dressed in a raincoat and flat cap, was a less disturbing version of his monotonous, glassy-eyed bore E L Wisty, already known to TV viewers. Dud, in a mackintosh and flat cap, was his twitchy friend.

The staging was simplicity itself. The two sat at a pub table, nursing pints of ale. There was little 'script', just header points around which the pair extemporised. Pete told Dud how he was being pestered by Betty Grable. Dud retorted with tales of how he'd found 'bloody Anna Magnani' in a see-through blouse, up to her knees in rice in his kitchen. Pete then explained how he'd heard a 'tap, tap, tap at the bloody window pane' one night earlier in the week and found 'bloody Greta Garbo', naked but for a see-through nightie and dark glasses, and had had to smash her away with a broomstick. Finally, Dud declared that he'd found Jane Russell stark naked in his bed just the other night and had thrown her down the stairs shouting, 'Get out of here, you hussy!', chucking her bra and gauze panties after her. There was even value in the pay-off, the two departing for another night at the pictures.

'Sex Fantasies' was a triumph of surrealism and improvisation, a piece that brought tears to the eyes of the audience both in the studio and at home – and also to Moore. Cook had a way of delivering his words while staring straight into the eyes of his partner. When he sensed a crack in his oppo's defences he enjoyed prising it wide. To see Dudley Moore flummoxed into stifled hysteria by an exquisite Cook ad lib is to witness one of the pure joys of comedy.

If *Not Only... But Also* (twenty-two editions, 1965–70) had just had Pete and Dud it would still be labelled a great show. As it was, this crowning glory of the Cook and Moore partnership rejoiced in a rich fund of sketches with an unlimited range of scenarios. It wasn't an early *Fast Show* but an extension of revue – a sketch, a song, a film, almost in rotation. Surreal, inventive, endlessly varied, it had many fine moments: sketches like 'Father and Son', 'Bo Duddley', 'Superthunderstingcar', more Streeb-Greebling interviews, music, poetry, trampolining nuns and much else. And at its heart were the Pete and Duds, masterpieces of ad lib artistry, a dreamlike tapestry of ideas, often drawing on the names and places of Dudley's Dagenham youth. Pete, the tall one, was dominant, making outrageous assertions with the buoyed poise of a fool who will not be denied. Dud, the small one, was an even more uninformed idiot, spasmatically hanging on his friend's words and making heroic efforts to illuminate or extend them. Gloriously working-class, dangerously ignorant about the weighty topics they chose to discuss, they were obsessed with women and their 'busty substances'. Pete's ideal, he informed Dud, was 'Audrey Hepburn with Jayne Mansfield overtones'.

'Art Gallery' is perhaps their finest sketch. Sitting down to eat their sandwiches, the pair evaluate what they've seen. They ponder why da Vinci's *Cartoon* doesn't strike them as funny. They formulate a mathematical equation: cost of painting divided by number of nudes equals amount of taxpayer's money per nude. They decide that the sign of a good painting is when the eyes follow you round the room; putting a nude painting to the test, they walk in opposite directions. Pete considers that this will make things tricky for the bottoms; Dud, twitching and blinking, pronounces that the bottoms would 'divide up

---

Overleaf: *Dagenham dialogue: Pete and Dud indulge their sex fantasies, 1965*

among themselves'. And of course, along the way, deviating delightfully from the rehearsed dialogue and fixing his friend with another challenging stare, Cook managed to reduce Moore to a spluttering heap.

Asked by *Radio Times* in 1965 to describe one another, Cook called Moore 'a cuddly bundle of fun' and Moore called Cook 'a long, gangling streak of cynicism'. This was no usual show-business double act. Their contemporaries – Morecambe and Wise, Mike and Bernie Winters – were reaping a big-money, small-screen reward for years of slogging around the halls. Cook and Moore were men of wry humour and a university education. The son of a diplomat, Cook was a devastatingly original humorist, the Noël Coward of his generation, a sharp wit who never did 'stand-up' and was at his best in unscripted situations. A 5ft 2in working-class boy with a club-foot, Moore was to his millions of admirers an utterly delightful man, a magnet for women, a comic of impish geniality who brought to his work the immaculate timing of the virtuoso jazz musician. Theirs was a complex marriage, simultaneously equal and unequal, certainly enjoyed and certainly endured. When going well it soared; when going badly a long separation – a divorce, essentially – ensued.

They made no more *Not Only... But Also* after 1970. It was time to move on, but neither knew where. Cook was starting to drink heavily, becoming unreliable and hurtful to his comedy partner. Soon they were stuck together on a long stage tour – their London show *Behind the Fridge* travelled to America as *Good Evening* – during which the relationship became strained to breaking point. At this time, fascinatingly, Pete and Dud suddenly re-emerged in more loutish – indeed brutal – form, as Derek and Clive. The names, they said, arrived randomly, although Derek was Dudley and Clive was Cook. Pete had once told Dud (in the sketch 'On Sex') that the worst word in the world was 'ba-stard', affirming, 'I knew it was filthy but didn't know how to use it'. Clive, and Derek, certainly did, as well as every other colourful obscenity in the English language, and they were fired with the full range of weaponry, from subtlety to sledgehammer. The f-word and c-word are more commonly broadcast today, but in the 1970s their shock value was tremendous. Not that the comedy of Derek and Clive – three albums and a film showing the making of the third – wasn't funny: the first album, especially, was at times as surreal in scope as Pete and Dud at their best. But after this the high points became fewer, the enterprise peaking in quality long before it ended.

With that end, Cook and Moore went their separate ways, Peter deeper into the bottle, Dudley to Hollywood, where he shone brightly but briefly as a superstar and sex symbol. Peter later reflected that, in Dudley, he had enjoyed 'a tremendous time' with a 'perfect comedy partner'. On a good day, Dudley would have echoed the sentiment.

We know where they are now. In 'Pete and Dud in Heaven' (1966) we saw them tramping the celestial pathway, their once grubby rain attire gleaming white, finding it a drab and boring place. (Pete: 'Is what I've been good for all my life? It's more like Liberace's bedroom.') Dud will be pouring Pete a nice cup of tea, the thin air will echo to the talk of Aunt Dolly, Mrs Woolley and Roger Braintree, and paradise will be convulsed with laughter as Cook and Moore navigate their unpredictable way through another blissful Dagenham Dialogue.

Private Eye
Craig Brown

Boasting to a child is always a mistake. A couple of years ago I bragged to my nine-year-old son, with the pride of a regular contributor, that *Private Eye* had just published its thousandth issue.

'So?' he replied with a sneer. '*Beano*'s on its three thousandth.'

The comparison was fair enough. The two magazines – or perhaps one should say the two comics – have much in common. Both deal in jokes. Both glorify mischief at the expense of responsibility. Both demonise the adult world so that, on a blind tasting, it would be hard to tell the difference between, say, Teacher of the Bash Street Kids and Alastair Campbell, or Sir Jimmy Goldsmith and Dennis the Menace's slipper-wielding dad. Both magazines relish nicknames: indeed, as far as I know the real names of most of the Bash Street Kids have never been disclosed, while in his heyday, Sir James could boast a good half-dozen, including Sir Jams, Sir James Goldfinger and Sir Jammy Fishpaste.

Both are printed on very cheap paper, reinforcing the frisson of there being something a little *samizdat* about them. Both are uniquely and inescapably British: even in the USA there is no equivalent of *Private Eye*, and American comics consist either of superheroes battling for world peace or cutesy, kooky kids who end up telling their moms just how much they really, really love them.

And both *Beano* and *Private Eye* consist of what is generally thought to be 'schoolboy humour'. 'The public-school boys who ran the *Eye* never grew up,' wrote one of the magazine's severest critics over a decade ago. '… They still offer obscenity, scurrility and libel, which may appeal especially to the younger reader, but over twenty-five years there has been a surfeit of it. Enough is enough… It is funny, too often, at someone else's expense.'

This particular critic was the late Robert Maxwell (aka the Bouncing Czech and Cap'n Bob), writing in 1986 after winning £55,000 in libel damages from *Private Eye*. Since then, Maxwell's reputation has taken a plunge, but this is no reason not to take his criticisms on board, as it were.

Schoolboyish or not? Certainly, when I first started reading *Private Eye*, I was a thirteen-year-old schoolboy (only two or three years out of *Beano*, I now realise). Looking back on those first issues that I read, I feel slightly bemused by what they could have meant to me. The cast list is as weird and wonderful, not to mention as incomprehensible, as *The Faerie Queene*. Allan 'Plug Em' Hall, Lady Magnesia Freelove, Peter Jaybotham, Piranha Teeth Stevens, Alan Watneys, Yvonne, Perishing Worthless, Glenda Slag, Lunchtime O'Booze: who *were* all those bizarre hobgoblins, and why was I, a thirteen-year-old schoolboy with no knowledge of their real-life counterparts, so endlessly fascinated by them?

Looking through *Private Eye*'s 250th issue, dated Friday 16 July 1971 – roughly the moment I signed on as a reader – I feel at a similar remove from these characters, many of them now dead or forgotten, as I must have felt then, yet their names still possess the same magnetic power.

In the 'Grovel' column, the short-sighted political editor of *The Times* is reported as having approached a woman at a party thrown by Norman St John Stevas. 'And what is a sweet young thing like you doing at a party like this?' he purred into her ear, only to be informed that the lady he was addressing was Princess Margaret. In the 'TV Topics' column by Lunchtime O'Views, a repeat of the disparaged *The First Churchills* series is held up as evidence of 'the depths of mediocrity to which the BBC has sunk'.

A correspondent on the letters page writes to congratulate Mr Auberon Waugh on his observation that 'Grocer' Heath's habit of defecating in public while on board *Morning Cleoud* [sic] may be a sign of incipient megalomania, citing Louis XIV and Cardinal Wolsey as earlier examples of this syndrome. A Heath cartoon depicts a couple watching Robin Day chairing a Common Market debate on television. 'If we go in,' says the husband, 'at least there won't be any more programmes about whether we should or not.'

The adolescent schoolboy tends to see grown-ups as gargoyles. It is a way of viewing the all-powerful adult world that makes it at the same time more grotesque and easier to fathom. *Private Eye* offers, as Maxwell suggested, a schoolboy vision, but it is a vision that springs from the same source as *Alice in Wonderland* and Punch and Judy and the poems of Edward Lear. And *Private Eye*'s particular genius has been to shape an alternative universe so mesmerising that its real-life victims seem ineluctably drawn into it, gradually metamorphosing into their own caricatures. All those toytown characters I read about as a schoolboy in the Seventies – Stonehouse, Thorpe, Nixon, Goldsmith, Kagan, the Dirty Digger – now seem ever more closely to resemble the images created for them by *Private Eye*. And even poor old Robert Maxwell will be remembered not, I suspect, as the benevolent international powerbroker he was so keen to become, but as the essentially ludicrous Cap'n Bob, the Bouncing Czech.

In this way, *Private Eye* resembles a magical doll's-house in which the schoolboy movement of each doll is eerily replicated in the real world beyond. Thus, Tony Blair is becoming increasingly like the happy-clappy control-freak vicar of the 'St Albion Parish News' column, and those who have seen Denis and Margaret Thatcher recently tell me that they now appear to be enacting their roles direct from the 'Dear Bill' column.

When John Major first became Prime Minister, I remember thinking that this time *Private Eye* had got it wrong, and that his caricature as a gawky Adrian Mole figure would never stand the test of time. I sensed that within a few months of being in Number 10 he would surely acquire a gravitas and *savoir faire* that would render his Mole-ish persona redundant. But no – he, too, was doomed to be shaped by satire: by the end of his term he seemed every bit as awkward and unsuitable as he had at the beginning.

Along with the forces of conservatism, one of Mr Blair's particular targets since assuming power has been those he describes as 'the cynics'. Let us hope that *Private Eye* continues to give him cause to reflect that cynicism has never been so buoyant. In fact, it is the one sport at which we British truly excel.

PRIVATE EYE

No. 756   FRIDAY 7 DECEMBER 1990   70p

Schoolboy humour? Private Eye *front cover: 7 December 1990*

Round the Horne
Jonathon Green

'Ladies and Gentlemen – the show that makes you clench your teeth – and fling them at the radio set – *Round the Horne*.'

They are, alas, all dead now: Barry Took and Marty Feldman who wrote the scripts for four series – sixty-six thirty-minute shows in all – Hugh Paddick, Betty Marsden and Kenneth Williams, who played the stock characters whose (mis)adventures continued week upon week, and that other Kenneth – Horne, he who gave it its name. Together with Bill Pertwee they embodied *Round the Horne*, broadcast on the BBC's Light Programme every Sunday lunchtime from 1964 to 1969. Golden ages are a dangerous concept, but the show's immense popularity at the time – and a continuing reputation reflected in the half-million-plus cassettes sold in the last ten years – renders it a true contender for such encomia.

The Sixties' BBC was, of course, no longer that of Lord Reith's Calvinistic didacticism. The 'wireless' had given way to the American 'radio', and those who enjoyed it were now just 'listeners', abbreviated from the 'listeners-in' of pre-war days. And nomenclature aside, its liberal Director-General, Hugh Greene, to the rabid outrage of such as Mary Whitehouse with her fantasies of theocratic censorship, ensured that the Corporation, once the Establishment par excellence, was imbued with the new atmosphere of irreverence that, however gradually, was transforming the society to which it broadcast. The obvious home for such irreverence was television, epitomised by the youthful satirists of *That Was the Week That Was*, but over at what was not yet known as 'steam radio' Horne and his crew could be heard waging their own, somewhat gentler siege of the status quo.

Unlike *TW3*, *Round the Horne* was no novelty. To borrow such biblical imagery as might suit Broadcasting House: in the beginning, that is 1943, was the services show *Merry-Go-Round* and its fictional RAF base, *Much Binding in the Marsh* (stars: Horne and Richard 'Stinker' Murdoch, plus Sam Costa and Maurice Denham, who themselves had featured in another top wartime show, *ITMA*); and *Much Binding* (from the RAF slang *bind*, to bore) begat *Beyond Our Ken* (Horne, plus Williams, Paddick, Marsden, Ron Moody, Patricia Lancaster and Stanley Unwin); and *Beyond Our Ken*, which ran from 1958 to 1964, begat *Round the Horne*.

Kenneth Horne had been plucked from wartime service in the RAF to make his first radio appearance in the series *Ack-Ack Beer Beer*. In 1943, as an announcer on the Overseas Recorded Broadcasting Service, he met Richard Murdoch, and together they wrote *Much Binding in the Marsh*. The show would continue into peacetime, running until 1953. It was perhaps fitting that Horne, who would maintain the role of 'straight man' no matter what the script, combined radio stardom with a variety of 'straight' jobs: among them

chairman of Chad Valley Toys and a director of Triplex Safety Glass. This business career was halted when in 1958 he suffered a stroke, temporarily losing the power of speech. As he recovered, he devised a new show: *Beyond Our Ken*. He would never return to the boardroom, becoming instead one of radio's best loved stars; there would even be a TV show, *Horne A Plenty*, for Thames Television, but he was, and remained, a radio man.

Horne aside, top of the bill was undoubtedly Kenneth Williams, the affection for whose *RTH* work is rivalled only by memories of his roles in so many *Carry On* films. His regular characters included the libidinous folksinger Rambling Syd Rumpo (self-styled 'picturesque, homespun, folksy twit'), the fiendish Japanese supervillain Chou En Ginsberg MA (Failed), and J Peasmould Gruntfuttock, a Whitehouse-derisory campaigner for more sex and violence in the media. After Williams came Hugh Paddick, *inter* much *alia* the 'Ageing Juvenile' Binkie Huckaback, playing endless two-handers as 'Charles' with Betty

The Round the Horne *team: Hugh Paddick, Kenneths Williams and Horne and Betty Marsden*

Marsden as 'Fiona'. Noël Coward at his most etiolated meets *Brief Encounter*: '*Charles*: I know. *Fiona*: I know you know. *Charles*: I know you know I know. *Fiona*: I know you know I know you know. *Charles*: I know.' Marsden, like Paddick a veteran of both 'legit' theatre and intimate revues whose career would take in both television and film, played a variety of women, notably Dame Celia Molestrangler and Daphne Whitethigh, a TV cook not wholly disassociated from that contemporary Nigella, Fanny Craddock (in *Beyond Our Ken* she had been simply Fanny Haddock). Finally, there was Bill Pertwee, whose cackhanded chatshow host Seamus Android reminded not a few of a then youthful Eamonn Andrews.

And, since without them there could have been no show, there were the writers: Barry Took and Marty Feldman. Took had worked on *BOK*, Feldman was the new boy. As Took has explained in his 1998 memoir of the show, 'our writing obsessions [. . .] were the music halls, the circus, seaside concert parties, and revolting old men'. They had met in the 1950s when both were essaying careers as music hall comedians. And while those efforts came to nothing, the experience would provide them with a vast database of comic material, both in the characters they encountered and in the language they overheard. All of this would find itself recycled in their scripts.

It is a truism that radio comedy is dependent on words. But few such comedies relished not merely words but language as did *Round the Horne*. *Beyond Our Ken* had shown the way; its successor was the apotheosis of the style. There were the funny names – such strange agglomerations as Cuckpowder, Boldwicket, Cornposture, Goosecreature or Dredgestrangler – there were the infinities of puns, of clichés that, taken literally, produced a whole new slant on their meaning; of catchphrases – no BBC comedy could exist without them (and still can't); of *double entendres*, camp and pure nonsense.

Of the last, the burden lay mainly on Williams' Syd Rumpo. His 'ganderbag' brimmed with bizarre 'folksongs', some way from Cecil Sharp House yet strangely feasible. 'Reg Pubes, Reg Pubes' runs his take on 'Widdecombe Fair', 'Lend me your great Nog, Rollock me fussett and grindle me nodes. For I want to go-o to Gangerpoke Bog, with – Len Possett, Tim Screevy, the reverend Phipps, Peg-leg Loombucket, Solly Levy, Ginger Epstein, Able Seaman Truefitt, Scotch Lil, Messrs Cattermole, Mousehabit, Neapthigh and Trusspot, solicitors ... and Uncle Ted Willis and all.' Such madness would become the standby of student imitators, the *Python* dead parrot sketch in embryo. At other times it is the Marx Brothers who seem to cast their shadow. '*Marsden*: Not so fast Mr Horne – Take this – *Horne*: Ow! *Marsden*: And that – *Horne*: Ooh! *Marsden*: And that – *Horne*: I can't take that. You've hardly got any left. *Marsden*: It's all right – I've got cupboards full at home and they'll only go stale.' Groucho and Chico would not, surely, have sneered.

As for *double entendres*, anyone could play. Whether it is Paddick and Marsden as Grand Prix commentator and pit-lane groupie ('*Marsden*: Oh Jock! It's close! It's close! It's desperately close! *Paddick*: Oh I beg your pardon, miss.') or Williams' poem of a prize marrow ('He took her down the garden path and showed it her with pride, / And when she saw the size of it the little lady sighed'), the Donald McGill seaside postcard influence is unmistakeable.

But of all the *RTH* humour, none equalled the strain of unashamed campery that ran through the show. Homosexuality would not be legalised until 1967, and the running references to the gay world, and its particular jargon, delighted both homosexuals who were already 'in', and a growing 'straight' public, who began to understand just what it was the team were going on about. At its simplest, there were the throwaway lines: 'Kenneth "Stinker" Williams, the fag with the filter tip…' and, in a reference to a well-known West End 'cottage': 'Kenneth Williams can be seen in "The Little Hut" in Leicester Square – Soap and towels, 3d extra.' Or Williams himself, admitting: 'Hello my dearios. And since we last met I've been where few men have been, and seen what few men have seen. And got off with a five pound fine'; or rounding off a 'patriotic little man' oration with the plea: 'We want 'omes. We fought for them. We deserve them.' Omes, for those who knew, meant men rather than dwellings. It is of course such terms as *ome*, or rather *omee*, taken from the gypsy-cum-theatrical-cum-gay language Polari, that lie at the heart of what would become *RTH*'s greatest attraction, the weekly appearance of that pair of 'resting professionals', Julian (Paddick) and Sandy (Williams), as they introduced 'Mr Horne' (utterly straight, even if some gay listeners believed that he had something going with 'Jules') to their latest attempt to make cash, simultaneously guying some 'swinging Sixties' fad, be it Bona Lallies, their bed and breakfast (housed in the bijou residence 'Duntrollin') or Bona Prods, their Soho film company. Jules and Sand – named for Julian Slade and Sandy Wilson, creators of the 1954 hit *The Boy Friend* – remain *RTH*'s finest hour, and Paddick's catchphrase 'Hello, I'm Julian and this is my friend, Sandy…' joined the immortals. And while many of their Polari terms may not have lasted – they were already a century-plus old in the Sixties – *butch* and *naff* (or *naph* as the scripts spell it) entered the mainstream slang vocabulary.

In 1969, when Kenneth Horne's fatal heart attack brought his eponymous show to an abrupt end, *RTH* was riding as high as ever. Yet real media power had shifted from radio to television – *Monty Python* had been launched, and such classics as *Steptoe and Son* and *Till Death Us Do Part* were already staples – and even *RTH* might not have been able to resist the new order. As it is, the show went out, and has stayed, at the top.

Spitting Image
Robin Oakley

Irreverence was the keynote of *Spitting Image*, the show that didn't give a damn. Whether it was the Pope unsuccessfully practising miracles in a Vatican broom cupboard, Archbishop George Carey seeking to modernise by substituting a tambourine for the cross as the new logo of the Anglican church or a bearded figure of God singing jingles about his failures in making the world, nothing was too sacred to be sent up. Nor was any image too vulgar for the programme makers to use, not even the acne-faced snooker player who directed balls into the pocket with pus squirted from his facial spots.

The age of deference for the royal family surely died during the eight years from 1984 to 1992 when up to 12 million viewers tuned in every Sunday night to see such scenes as the Queen sniffing her son's discarded underpants while she and Prince Philip berated a bed-lounging Prince Edward for his failure to get a job. There was a money-crazed Fergie charging her parents-in-law £20 a head for visiting and the whole royal 'firm' donning stocking masks to become bank robbers when evicted for failing to pay their poll tax after the Queen Mother had gambled away Buckingham Palace on a *Sporting Life* tip.

My own favourite among the running gags, such as those playing on Cliff Richard's much-prolonged virginity or a gold lamé-suited Jimmy Saville's attempts to escape being locked in a padded cell, was the one of Prince Charles as a whingeing taxi-driver, boring his passengers silly with an endless stream of complaints: 'Why does that Ian McCaskill tell us what the weather's been today? That's not weather forecasting. And another thing: why can't they fit shades to keep the sun off the windows in cash machines?' As if he would need one.

There was sharp, near-the-knuckle comment too on issues like the sale of kidneys for transplants. And the parodies of advertisements were spot on, like the spoof part-sales magazine *Macho Moron*, incorporating *Bullet in the Groin* magazine: 'It helps you build up your own mad fantasy world… Week Two: put on a bandanna and combat fatigues and prowl your bedsit. Week Three: go out and shoot up the local supermarket… For budding psychopaths everywhere… Free grenade with next week's issue.'

The musical skits were always good, especially a Loadsamusic take-off of the self-consciously downmarket Nigel Kennedy:

Supporting Aston Villa to show that I'm not posh
And dropping all me aitches to help bring in the dosh.

Politicians on the whole probably didn't suffer too badly from being guyed on *Spitting Image*, which tended in most cases to reinforce impressions already held. The public knew that Norman Tebbit, the Chingford Skinhead, was a tough politician who gave no quarter long before *Spitting Image* presented him in leathers swinging a bicycle chain. Margaret

Thatcher was already perceived as a bossy, domineering figure long before her shrill beak-nosed presentation on the Sunday night show. Indeed, she even used to joke about it herself, sweeping into a cabinet committee one day and declaring, 'I've only got time to explode and have my way'. And Michael Heseltine was happy enough to play up to his image as a wild-haired Tarzan-like figure, later entitling his autobiography *Life in the Jungle*. He says: 'In a sense *Spitting Image* made me. I was an obscure member of the government, a common or garden cabinet minister, and suddenly wherever I went it was Hezza or Michael. I was a celebrity.'

One who did lose out from his presentation on *Spitting Image* was David Steel, leader of the Liberal Party when they were working in the Alliance with the Social Democrats, led by David Owen. Steel, a shrewd parliamentarian who could hold his own in any political company, was depicted as a pathetic little figure tucked into Owen's top pocket, dominated and doing his bidding. One typical sketch had the two of them in bed together:

Steel: David, after we have merged, what shall we call our new party?
Owen: I propose we take one part of your party's name and one part of my party's name.
Steel: What bit of your party's name will you take, David?
Owen: Social Democratic.
Steel: Then what part of my party's name will you take, David?
Owen (sneering): Party.
Steel (looking crestfallen): Very well, David.

Over a period such a depiction did do Steel harm, leading one commentator to summarise the relationship as 'David Steel hitches lifts, David Owen drives trucks'.

On the principle that any publicity is good publicity, politicians in general affected not to mind their portrayal. Certainly, many of them were avid viewers. In his days as Chief Secretary to the Treasury, when his London home was a flat in Stockwell, John Major used to drive back from Huntingdon on a Sunday evening, anxious to get there in time to watch *Spitting Image*. But biographer Anthony Seldon says that as Prime Minister the thin-skinned Major loathed the programme. When he was first in Downing Street it had him wearing an antenna through which he was controlled by Margaret Thatcher. Later he was shown as a sad and lonely figure in monochrome grey, speaking in a strangled monotone and counting tinned peas on his plate. Margaret Thatcher never watched the programme and I doubt if two former home secretaries, Labour's Roy Hattersley and Conservative Kenneth Baker, chose to buy their puppets when they were eventually auctioned off at Sotheby's. Baker was depicted as a slug, Hattersley as a blubbermouth cascading spittle. But in essence being caricatured on the programme was a sign that you had made it.

Overleaf: *Latex alter egos: Robin Day, Prince Philip, Margaret Thatcher and Vincent Price, with voices*

With its gloriously disrespectful latex puppets, controlled by two operators using steel cables and air bulbs, *Spitting Image* provided a genuine contribution to the visual arts, combining physical embodiments of the savage caricature of Gillray and Steadman with the kind of political satire pioneered in Britain by *Beyond the Fringe* and *That Was the Week That Was* and continued, most recently, by *Bremner, Bird and Fortune*. It was the creation of Peter Fluck and Roger Law, contemporaries at Cambridge School of Art, where they met *Beyond the Fringe* star Peter Cook. He employed Law as an illustrator on projects like *Private Eye* and a political comic strip in the *Observer*. Fluck and Law, who formed a partnership spooneristically entitled Luck and Flaw, began creating sculpted images for newspapers and magazines like the *Sunday Times* and the *Economist*, and were encouraged to launch the *Spitting Image* project by Martin Lambie-Nairn, a designer at London Weekend Television.

Several backers were apparently exhausted before the £150,000 pilot was finally completed, and in its first season, concentrating almost entirely on politics, *Spitting Image* did comparatively poorly in the ratings. But the programme was nursing some precocious talents, with the puppets' voices provided by such as Rory Bremner, Harry Enfield, Steve Nallon, Jan Ravens, Enn Reitel, Steve Coogan and John Sessions. When it was broadened to caricature showbiz and sporting figures too it became a national 'Did you see?' phenomenon.

I don't know which of them used to 'do' David Attenborough, but I will always treasure the sketch which had him voicing over pictures of a giant panda with his usual hushed, churchlike reverence: 'Secretive. Elusive. For centuries at one with nature. Yet now the panda's peace has been shattered. As man ravages the panda's habitat, the threat of extinction looms…' Then, without a switch of tone: 'And, quite frankly, who gives a monkey's? For what does it do? It sits there all day on its fat arse nicking bamboo shoots. All we're talking about is some silly fat Herbert who does sweet FA…' If you could get away with mocking David Attenborough and nature before a British audience, you really had got it made. *Spitting Image* could, and did.

Steptoe and Son
Graham McCann

If you want to understand both the nature and the history of the great British brand of situation comedy, then *Steptoe and Son*, above all others, is the show you need to study. This was the show that had it all. It was also the show that had it first.

The handful of small-screen sitcoms that came before it – such as *The Army Game* (1957), *The Larkins* (1958), *Here's Harry* (1960) and, most memorable of all, the wonderful *Hancock's Half-Hour* (which made the transition from radio to television in 1956) – were far stronger on the 'com' than the 'sit', containing plenty of light but precious little shade. *Steptoe and Son* changed that. It brought to the genre a much deeper sense of self-belief.

The transformation happened, indirectly, because of Tony Hancock. When, in 1961, he decided to end his decade-long association with his two writers, Ray Galton and Alan Simpson, he handed them, quite unwittingly, the opportunity to progress beyond the limitations of his own 'star personality' style of sitcom.

Invited soon after the split by Tom Sloan, BBC TV's then Head of Light Entertainment, to write ten unrelated half-hour pieces under the *Comedy Playhouse* banner, they saw the proposed series as a golden opportunity to graduate from serving comic performers to guiding serious actors, and to start creating the kind of scripts that could move as well as amuse. They duly proceeded to prove themselves right.

The fourth show in the sequence, entitled 'The Offer', focused on the peculiarly ambivalent bond between an elderly father, Albert Steptoe, and his middle-aged son, Harold. When it was broadcast, on 5 January 1962, its impact was both immediate and immense. 'Of course, you realise what you've written, don't you?' a delighted Tom Sloan asked the two writers, before going on to answer on their behalf: 'It's marvellous, it's a series.'

Indeed it was, as well as rather more than that: this beautifully written and smartly performed sitcom went on to run for eight series, from 1962 to 1974, regularly attracting audiences of 20 million or more, and spawned two movie spin-offs, six radio series, one touring show and a hugely successful American television adaptation by the name of *Sanford and Son*. So great was its popularity that an episode scheduled for the evening of the 1964 general election was delayed (at the request of an opposition leader fearful of its damaging effect on voter turnout) until after polling had ended.

What, then, was so special about *Steptoe and Son*? First of all, there was the realism (in the conservative terms of the television comedy of the time) of the setting: it took viewers away from the lace-curtained cosiness of previous sitcoms and into the gritty, grubby, gloomy working-class milieu of a rag-and-bone man's ramshackle home in Oil Drum Lane, Shepherd's Bush. Second, it featured a daringly dark, tragicomic 'trapped

Bringing real life to the sitcom: Wilfrid Brambell as Steptoe and Harry H Corbett as Son

relationship' between a dour, habit-hardened proletarian and a socially sanguine, would-be *petit bourgeois*. Third, it was based on the kind of clever but compassionate writing that was capable of pathos and poignancy as well as sauce and slapstick. And finally, instead of resting on certain pre-existing comic personae, its two central characters were brought to life by serious, stage-trained actors (dapper, Dublin-born Wilfrid Brambell as the scruffy and irascible Albert, and moody, serious-minded Harry H Corbett as the hopelessly idealistic and pathetically snobbish Harold).

It struck a chord with the British people. Appearing at a time when new tensions were emerging between the young and the old, especially in terms of the growing differences between their respective cultural tastes, lifestyles and social aspirations, the world of *Steptoe and Son* was one with which all ages and classes could identify.

It was a very British world: a world populated by stubbornly proud traditionalists and increasingly exasperated innovators. As a furious Harold exclaimed, after seeing yet another plan for progress sabotaged by his craftily conservative father: 'You frustrate me in everything I try to do. You are a dyed-in-the-wool, fascist, reactionary, squalid little know-your-place, don't-rise-above-yourself, don't-get-out-of-your-hole, complacent little turd!' (An outburst that failed to provoke his father into uttering any sharper response than: 'What d'yer want for yer tea?')

It was a world in which there was always a ready putdown to puncture any pretension. If, for example, Harold's language grew too highfalutin ('Your mere presence tends to impinge upon my aesthetic pleasures and moments of relaxation'), Albert could be relied on to offer a plainer translation ('In other words: I get on your tits!'). Similarly, whenever Harold's dreams of a better life drifted too far from his working-class reality – such as when he imagined transforming his shared junkyard hovel into a fashionable salon, a 'powerhouse of intellectual thought' so full of 'choice wines, superb food and elegant conversation' that the likes of 'C P Snow and Bertrand Russell will be busting a gut to get in' – vulgar Albert would always step in to bring him crashing back down to earth: 'Oh *yeah*! There'll be *plenty* for them to do *here*: table tennis, rat hunting. I can see you all now, going for long tramps across the yard deep in intellectual conversation and horse manure.'

It was also a world in which, when it most mattered, no one, being typically British, could bring themselves to say what they really felt. Albert would do his best to hurt Harold – 'You can't *wait* to hear the first shovelful of dirt hit the coffin, can you? I wouldn't be mourned, I know that. You'd be *dancing* on my grave!' – and Harold would do his best to hurt Albert – 'Oh, you *poor* old man! You ain't got nothing to live for, have you? Here, cut your throat, put yourself out of your misery!' – because both men hoped that the show of hate would help hide the love.

All of British life was there, at its most intimate and essential, in *Steptoe and Son*, and that was why it made us blush almost as easily and as often as it made us laugh. Look closely at any of the key sitcoms that have come since – from *Till Death Us Do Part* to *The Office* – and the dirty fingerprints of *Steptoe and Son* will not be hard to spot.

If one seeks to reach down to the roots of sitcom cruelty, one will find oneself back at the end of the very first *Steptoe* episode, watching Albert (just after poor, humiliated Harold has slammed the door in the face of his supposedly insensitive hour-late date) sneak up to the living-room clock, slip the big hand back to its proper hour, and then smile to himself in triumph. If one attempts to trace the way back to the earliest days of sitcom compassion, one will end up at more or less the same place, and re-encounter the episode of *Steptoe* in which Harold's upmarket birthday treat for his father (taking in a quick trip to a West End cocktail bar – '*What?* Seven and six for a bleedin' fruit salad?' – a screening of Fellini's *8½* – 'Maybe it's his hat size' – and then a slap-up supper at a Chinese restaurant – '*Eeeuugh!*') fails dismally to draw their two lonely outlooks any closer together.

Steptoe and Son was also, of course, very, very funny, but it was never funny in a simplistic or shallow way. It succeeded in making us laugh because it had already taken the time and trouble to make us believe. Aside from the solitary 'You *dirty* old man!' there were no real catchphrases, nor was there any reliance on wildly improbable plots or clumsily signposted gags: there were just two characters who rang true, who made sense, and who seemed just as flawed and fragile and foolish as the rest of us.

It was not the show that brought the sitcom to life; it was the show that brought real life to the sitcom. None of us, even now, is very far from someone like Steptoe or his son. Just look around you. Just look inside.

That Was the Week That Was
Simon Hoggart

Towards the end of 2002 the BBC held a lavishly catered party at Television Centre – all champagne and those mini-fish-and-chip things in newspaper – to celebrate the fortieth anniversary of *That Was the Week That Was*. For those of a nostalgic disposition – I was seventeen when the show began – it was a wonderfully evocative affair. The show was so important – probably more influential than any other British television programme – that it's hard to remember that its total run lasted hardly more than a year. It was even on a long summer holiday when the Profumo affair broke, and in the autumn of 1963 the BBC seized gratefully on the general election, due the following year, as an excuse to cancel it for good.

Only two of the original cast, Willie Rushton and Roy Kinnear, have died since 1962, and the rest – David Frost, Lance Percival, Millicent Martin, Kenneth Cope and David Kernan – were all present and performing at the 2002 bash. Bernard Levin was there, ill and unable to speak, but still capable of taking a graceful bow when Frost paid tribute to him.

Millicent Martin sang a topical song, and showed that age – and her spell as Daphne's magnificently vulgar mother in *Frasier* – have left her voice in almost as good shape as it was. They showed the classic sketches, such as Gerald Kaufman's biting jibes at the silent MPs and at the *Sunday Express*'s Crossbencher, whose predictions were delivered with magisterial aplomb but had an unfortunate habit of being entirely inaccurate. This item led to one of the many kerfuffles which surrounded the show. Crossbencher had finished his last column with a confident claim that the then ailing Labour leader Hugh Gaitskell would soon be up on his feet again. Frost looked into the camera, and said 'Sorry, Hugh!' Within three weeks Gaitskell was dead.

And we caught again the famous embarrassing conversation between Martin and Kinnear, sitting in a café, that ends with her shouting at him: 'Yer fly is open!' This had seemed immensely daring at the time, though less so in the twenty-first century, when a Channel 4 sitcom can show people having oral sex.

At one point the surviving cast performed a series of short gags about the news of the previous week, just as they did in the original, with each mini-sketch forming a brief conversation between them as they sat in line at a desk. This was less successful and fell rather flat, though the jokes were no doubt as good as they would have been four decades earlier. But the world has moved on. *TW3*, as it was always called, created the present genre of quickfire political humour, and now everyone does it: Rory Bremner, *The News Quiz*, *Have I Got News for You*, *Dead Ringers*, *2DTV*; even Ned Sherrin, the begeter of *TW3*,

---

Looking as if he was born on TV: David Frost as TW3 *anchorman, 1963*

starts his *Loose Ends* show on Radio 4 with a topical monologue. There aren't enough jokes to go round.

It was very different forty years before. Nothing remotely like it had ever been seen on British television. *TW3* was irreverent, satirical, and cared nothing at all for authority or accepted practice. It was open-ended and, deceptively, looked unstructured. Its very casualness seemed an unspoken rebuke to existing light entertainment shows, with their precise timing, conventional rituals and whiskery old ideas for jokes. It loathed the elderly clichés about British life as reflected in British television. For instance, one rule was that television had to pretend that it wasn't television at all; the intrusion of a camera or a microphone boom was highly unprofessional. Sherrin shot live, and didn't care if the audience saw the nuts and bolts of the technology. The show had to be fast and pacey, never smooth and slick.

TW3 did not arrive in a vacuum. The revue *Beyond the Fringe* had appeared at the Edinburgh festival in 1960; it included Peter Cook's famous Harold Macmillan impression, which seems mild enough now, but was astonishing then. The first edition of *Private Eye* appeared the following year, just after the Establishment Club, which specialised in satire, had opened in Soho. The notion that it was television's job to give politicians a hard time was not entirely new either. Robin Day had already started his acerbic interviews, so different from the traditional 'we are grateful to you for coming into the studio to explain your bill, Minister' approach. Frankie Howerd, the comedian who restarted his career with a stand-up turn on *TW3*, got a huge laugh when he talked about Day's 'cruel glasses', and the phrase passed into the language. All British entertainment was changing fundamentally: The Beatles' first hit, 'Love Me Do', entered the charts in December 1962, the month *TW3* premiered.

Sherrin had worked on *Tonight*, the nightly magazine programme which, though not a comedy show, gave a light and less respectful twist to the news. He also wanted to catch some of the flavour of the late-night American programmes, which might as well have been broadcast on the moon for all the influence they had on British TV. He gathered the team by watching them in various clubs and nightspots. Millicent Martin, the only regular woman, thought the show had few prospects, and regretted turning down a panto in Bromley. David Frost, who modelled himself on Peter Cook, had been performing at The Blue Angel in London; in Sherrin's version, his act was so poor he had to beg the manager to let him back onstage. But Frost, who looks now as if he had been born on television, turned out to be a supremely confident performer, unfazed by whatever the live broadcast threw up, relishing the danger.

There had to be two pilot shows before the BBC felt confident enough to go ahead. The whole thing had a scary, seat-of-the-pants feel. Bernard Levin, who did a regular slot in which he abused various groups in the studio – farmers and public relations officers, for example – was once punched, on air, by the husband of a woman whose play he had panned. Scripts were sometimes commissioned on the Saturday itself; taxis were kept running as final lines were written. Lance Percival's topical calypso included riffs about items which had just appeared on the show.

The first broadcast was on 25 November 1962 and came at the very end of the BBC's broadcasting for that night. The team had hoped for an audience of around a million; in fact three and a half million watched, and the *Sunday Telegraph* managed to run a rave review the following morning. As word spread, and the pubs were famously emptied, the audience rose to 12 million – with only three channels available, viewing figures were higher than now, but even so that was an astonishing success for such a late time slot.

Probably the most famous show of all, the one that cast *TW3*'s reputation in bronze, was the third, which ran on 8 December. It included the fly-buttons sketch; an attack on the nation's most popular musical writer, Lionel Bart, for alleged plagiarism; a Bernard Levin confrontation with just one man, the restaurateur Charles Forte; and most notorious of all, a sketch in which a group of cardinals, leaving the Vatican Council, sang '*Arriverderci, Roma*'. Not the most hilarious idea in the world, perhaps, but a signal that not even religion was exempt. Later, a consumer guide to religions, done in the style of *Which?* magazine, created even more fuss.

The received wisdom is that Britain was then a complacent society which needed an urgent kick up the backside. I don't think that's entirely right. My memory is that we were deeply troubled; aware that our international status had largely evaporated (Dean Acheson's line about Britain losing an empire and not yet having found a role came between the second and third shows) and that the defeated nations of Europe were beginning to overtake us. Yet at the same time there was a considerable amount of complacency left sloshing around, in society as a whole, not only in the political world, a sense that we had always done things in the same way and there was no need to change. *TW3* happily mocked even the smallest details of life, such as school textbooks. I remember joyfully watching Frost announcing with immense gravity, 'if you can imagine a pea placed on top of a grapefruit, that will give you some idea of what a beach ball would look like on the dome of St Paul's'.

Hugh Carleton Greene, the BBC's director general, had hoped *TW3* would recreate the great days of satire which flourished in Berlin during the 1930s. That, of course, had done nothing to stop the rise of Hitler. In the same way, *TW3* was a victim of its own success. Satire had become too powerful for its own good. If the government of the day had not had the Profumo scandal and had felt more secure, it might have brushed the show aside. As it was, the pressure on the BBC and the Governors grew stronger, and towards the end of 1963 it was announced that *TW3* would not return in 1964. A series of lesser versions, *Not So Much a Programme...* and *BBC-3* followed without creating remotely the same stir.

But that toothpaste would not go back in the tube. British television had changed forever. Would it have changed anyway, if Sherrin had never gathered his team? Probably; the pressures on the old social structures were too great. But not this suddenly, and nowhere near as effectively.

The Two Ronnies
Peter Vincent

'You've heard of a man being built like a Greek god? Here's a man built like a Greek restaurant.' So Ronnie Corbett introduces his co-star, Ronnie Barker, as another edition of *The Two Ronnies* begins. They seat themselves behind a news desk. 'I like this desk,' says Ronnie Corbett, 'you can't see that my feet don't touch the ground.' 'You can't see that my stomach does,' rejoins Barker.

Television stars do not age. The Ronnies look just as young and fresh as Laurel and Hardy. Talking about them compels the present tense. They're still on our screens, although the twelve series of *The Two Ronnies* were recorded between the years 1971 and 1987. The comparison with Laurel and Hardy is particularly apt. Stan and Ollie were not a true double act in the classic manner, with a straight man who proposed a serious idea and a comic who made a mess of it. They were both equally funny. So it is with the Ronnies.

The Rons are a complete contrast. RB is an actor. RC is a comic. Ronnie Corbett on screen has a distinct personality, a kind of intimate knowingness coupled with a delicate Scottish prudery. Ronnie Barker claims not to have a personality at all. He is a master of rapid and faultless delivery, someone who revels in language. Each is a paradox: RC is a small man with considerable authority, RB a large man, who is subtle and light on his feet.

Television is good on information. By seeming to be *au fait*, it claims a kind of spurious authority. 'We've just heard…' says David Frost, and we almost believe he *has* just heard it. He's connected with everything that's going on. In reality, 'We've just heard…' is the intro to a gag.

In this genre – born out of *The Frost Report* – comes the Two Ronnies' news desk which tops and tails every show. 'We've just heard that an elephant has done the ton on the M1… A man who committed an offence at Becher's Brook has asked for twenty-six other fences to be taken into consideration… And now an aria from the opera which tells of the sad honeymoon of "Eskimo Nell" – "You're Tiny and It's Frozen…"'

The point about the news items is that they have to *sound* like news items. Elegant circumlocution is the style. Anything crude and feisty has to be made official and anodyne. What's the weather in Lissingdown? Well, it's not going to be pissing down. It has to be 'rather wet' or 'inclement'. When *Not the Nine o'Clock News* mounted a very funny send-up of *The Two Ronnies* they rather missed the point about these prissy news items and made a joke about something that was already a joke. It's parody, you see… Oh, never mind.

The Two Ronnies is one of the last examples of a variety tradition. Each show has a guest singer, a musical finale provided by our heroes (remember *Romeo and Juliet* to the music of Sousa?), comedy sketches, two contrasting monologues and that joyous excursion from the studio, the filmed serial, such as the adventures of Piggy Malone and Charlie Farley (BA). Infinite variety – too expensive for this more streamlined age. (For 'streamlined' read 'cheap'.)

Jonathan Miller discusses the humour of Peter Cook and Dudley Moore, another duo without a straight man, in a sketch where a one-legged man is auditioning for the part of Tarzan. Peter Cook says to the hapless Dudley Moore: 'You only have the one leg, whereas it would be better to have at least two.' Miller points to the words 'at least', which imply that three legs would be even better. Implication is funnier than statement. Implying something leaves the audience something to work out. Laughter signifies the joy of having worked it out successfully. We understand… Join the club.

In a film item by Ronnie Barker, some gardeners are told to move a hole from one end of the garden to the other. They don't dig the hole in the new place and fill in the other one. Of course not. They've been told to move the hole itself so they gradually… You're ahead of me, aren't you? It's logic, but not as we know it. In another sketch, Ronnie Corbett finds himself in a restaurant which serves only rooks. You'd think that the waiter would be keenly promoting this extraordinary idea. Not in the least. Writer David Nobbs has the waiter running the place down. They only serve 'bloody awful tough old rooks'. A strange but wonderful world is not described but implied. Why on earth does the waiter stay there? For the same reason the gardeners move the hole. Within this different world it must be logical.

In another *Two Ronnies* sketch, a woman has kept her lover in the house by disguising him as the family dog. Ronnie Corbett was the dog, but just before the sketch began Ronnie Barker paraded a real dog in front of the studio audience. When we first saw Ronnie Corbett in his dog suit we thought it was the real dog. In the sketch, the lover is discovered because the dog has been smoking too much and sitting on the sofa watching telly. Far from being abashed, the lover complains that it's been a dog's life, he's only won a third prize at Crufts. A world is implied where a man dressed as a dog can do well at Crufts but *still* thinks he could have done better.

It's the distorting mirror that contrives to show us the truth – a mad world, my masters, but nonetheless illuminating. (Leave this stuff to Freud. *Ed.*) Sorry. Right. Ronnie Barker's monologues often feature a confident, well-presented spokesman. He is so suave and assured that for a moment we don't realise he's speaking complete nonsense. 'This is a very important point on the graph – because I can hang my umbrella on it.' So various are RB's characters that we sometimes forget this is his monologue spot. But he's an actor. This is not to be a stand-up routine. He's playing a role and following the first rule of comedy acting: he's playing it straight. Like Peter Sellers, he never comes on as himself. This is perhaps what he means when he says he doesn't have a personality.

Although Ronnie Corbett was always at ease doing the warm-up, Ronnie Barker had sharp antennae at all times for the mood of the studio audience. If a sketch didn't seem to

Overleaf: *It's goodnight from them: Ronnies Corbett and Barker at the news desk, 1978*

be going well, it was Ronnie Barker who would make a clumsy mistake and stop the recording. He apologises. The studio audience love it. They restart, with twice as many laughs. Not so clumsy after all.

Ronnie Corbett does his stand-up sitting down. He is always about to tell a joke, but he rambles. The digressions are the point. He talks about his size, his wife, the BBC canteen, the producer, who, in the best comic tradition, is a hopeless drunk. Only the main joke of the piece is as old as the hills – the older hills, that is. Whoops, there I go. Goodness. The style is catching.

The convention with many comics is to seem to make up their jokes as they go along. Who cares about the writers anyway? The Two Ronnies acknowledge that theirs was very much a writers' show. As many as fifty writers contributed the news items. Ronnie Barker in his guise of Gerald Wiley is himself a writer and is responsible for some of the best moments in the show, such as the famous 'Four Candles… Fork Handles' sketch. Wordplay is his forte. Even as a writer he's light on his feet. The name 'Wiley' is well chosen.

But I digress. Spike Mullins was the writer who created 'Ronnie in the Chair'. The tradition was extended happily by David Renwick. Ronnie 'Goliath' Corbett is at ease in the chair. He tells us modestly that he stands head and shoulders beneath other comics. In fact, he was once the ringmaster in a flea circus. He goes to the canteen, where the food is so old they have to put mothballs in the jacket potatoes. Good heavens, they're holding a mass for the trifle! Luckily the BBC has organised a mystery outing. For £6.50 you get a skateboard and a blindfold… The jokes in this paragraph are by David Renwick, a man who would never sue a fellow writer.

Off screen the contrast between the two stars is sharper. Ronnie Corbett is expansive, charming and generous. His care for fellow human beings is constantly projected into other places, other lives. In a social context he worries about the caterers, the washing up, the people in the other room. Ronnie Barker is much more private, extremely witty, always so many steps ahead that he seems out on his own. They're not a team so much as a very happy coincidence. As if to emphasise the fact, each has appeared in comedy without the other. *Porridge* has become a classic, perhaps because Fletcher is not unlike Ronnie Barker himself, shrewd, always that step ahead, wily – wily as Wiley, you might say. In *Sorry* Ronnie Corbett wears a wig to become Timothy Lumsden, who is a confection unlike Ronnie in almost every way. Another paradox! The actor plays himself, the comedian pays a part.

Times change. Picture postcards fade. The general shop in the 'Four Candles' sketch is itself a curling snapshot of a vanished world. Comedy has become cruder, verbally more violent. Inevitably *The Two Ronnies* seems mild, redolent of a more kindly era, suggestive but not obvious, satirical but not sneering. You could say they are the last bastion against the dumbing down of… 'Bulwarks!' I hear you cry. They are. They are comedy greats. Television has made them immortal. But just for now it's:

Goodnight from him – and it's goodnight from him.

Viz
Stephen Bayley

Viz is a cult magazine, but given its epically smutty character, you have to be awfully careful typing that four-letter word. To its readers *Viz* offers total immersion in a unique culture, whose unflinching vulgarity in fact disguises a sophisticated and selfconscious awareness. There is something distinctively British about this, as there is about the magazine's publishing history, which is an idiosyncratic blend of amateur genius and very clever business.

John Brown was managing director of Virgin Books. One day in 1984 he found himself in bed with 'flu and had nothing to do but watch television. He saw two Newcastle-upon-Tyne brothers, Chris and Simon Donald, then teenagers. They were wearing lab-coats and discussing, with mock seriousness, their new comic magazine, already becoming a minor phenomenon in the North-east. Brown was stirred from his stupor, so when a copy later landed on his desk his mind was prepared. He told me he immediately read the entire thing standing up. Then, he said, 'I went very quiet and still and thought "This is my future".'

Brown flew up to Teesside and did the deal. *Viz* was then selling about four thousand copies in pubs, but management was anarchic and they had managed a mere twelve issues in five years. Brown offered the Donalds £1,500 advance on each issue, did a distribution deal with the people who handled *Private Eye*, and they were in business. Brown decided to leave Virgin and take *Viz* with him, but he needed backers. He told Virgin's Richard Branson, 'I want £25,000 for 15 per cent'. Branson said, 'I'll give you £15,000 for 25 per cent'. It was very shrewd of both of them. Soon *Viz*'s circulation was up to 1.2 million and it was the third bestselling magazine in the country after *Radio Times* and *TV Times*.

Any sentient being living in Britain over the past twenty years has a *Viz* story. This is mine. It was Karlheinz Stockhausen's music agent who introduced me to *Viz*. This is wonderfully odd and in its hilarious inversion of normalcy entirely in the style of this remarkable publication. I mean: if the introduction had been made by some macho media hack paddling pissed in the shallow end of the gene pool, it would not have been surprising. But to have an urbane, cosmopolitan sophisticate, whose stock-in-trade is the discussion of serialised parameters, say to me, 'Look, here's this big red stonking hard thing you must read because it's very funny' was surreal. And true.

Viz, whose production standards are not very far north of a school magazine, and whose sense of decorum can be found way south, is a national treasure. Like great drama, movies and books, its cast of cartoon characters populates our imagination. Sid the Sexist, Roger Mellie the Man on Telly, the Fat Slags and Johnny Fartpants are now as real as Lorna Doone, James Bond and King Lear… with the added advantage of making us laugh.

It does no justice to the challenging rudeness, the magnificent offensiveness, the gutter-dwelling coprophilia, the unabashed disgustingness, the continuous insistence on transgression, the repulsive lack of tact of *Viz* to call it lavatory humour. It is not at all difficult to find lavatories with higher standards of sub-editing: I don't think *Viz* has any. In the magazine's remorseless commitment to scatological excess there is, however, a form of authentic excellence: a consistent commitment to extremes which none but a churl would disavow. It's difficult, even in these days of relaxed social norms, for many of us to say 'Here man, y' fuckin' radge, tek a chill pill', so it's nice to have a *Viz* character do it for us.

Viz has its own language, but what started as a folkloric lexicon – with the Donalds doing diligent pseudo-scholarly lexicography in Tyne and Tees bars – has acquired a demented creative energy of its own. The language is usually based on puerile metaphors. The Talmud uses architectural terms to describe the entrance to the female genitalia and so does *Viz*: thus, 'beef curtain'. In an appallingly funny illustration of the concept, *Viz* once showed two sheets of supermarket brisket hanging from a domestic pelmet to illustrate this affectionately smutty term for the intimidating *labia maiora*. This vocabulary of filth has been collected in a spin-off mock dictionary known as *Roger's Profanisaurus*, a schoolboyish take on *Roget's Thesaurus*, evoking the *Viz* favourite Roger Mellie the Man on Telly. In its crazy way, the *Profanisaurus* is a serious work which makes a genuine contribution to the study of language, deserving a place next door to Eric Partridge's epic *Dictionary of Historical Slang*, its entries revealing a dedication to obscenity that is profound and even inspiring.

The central proposition of *Viz* is that genitals, the acts of sexual connection and the processes and products of defecation are very funny. This, of course, is distinctively British. In his humourless way, Freud agreed. *Viz* exploits to the full the enormous vocabulary of low words provided by the theatre of the bed and the bog, but unlike academic lexicographers, the *Viz* team is also generating, in singular style, its own new material to add to the national word trove. While much of this is indubitably disgusting and crude, not to mention inelegant, the mysterious chemistry of *Viz* makes it somehow inoffensive.

In its uninhibited use of bawdy there is something pleasingly traditional about *Viz*. Curiously, swearing is not a human universal. The Japanese, for instance, tend not to, whereas the British have a reputation for doing it rather a lot, often in four letters. Joan of Arc's men called us the 'Goddems', because we were always saying 'God damn it!' More recently, our heroic rosbifs have been known as 'les fuckoffs'. There is a 308-page volume devoted exclusively to Shakespeare's word trove of insults ('puke-stocking' is a favourite of mine) and recently Jesse Sheidlower, an editor of *The Random House Historical Dictionary of American Slang* has been able to devote an entire book to The F-Word.

Besides sex and excretion, race, religion, deformity and nationality are recurrent professional concerns of the *Viz* editorial team. Naturally, this makes them vulnerable to criticism from the prim, grim armies of correctitude (who perhaps intuit that laughter is a condition of libertarian rebellion). But while it would be going too far to describe the

Lavatory humour minus the editing: Viz

anarchic filth of *Viz* as an agent of liberal change, it's a reasonable proposition to say that Sid the Sexist ('I've aalwez been a tit-man, like') has probably done more good for women's issues than any amount of grant-aided, index-linked, politically correct, subsidised, joyless feminist lobbying.

By 2000 *Viz* had peaked, with circulation settling at about 200,000. Production values had improved (a bit) and while the magazine was carrying full-page ads for international brands of coffee and cigarettes, a tradition of trenchant silliness was maintained with classifieds soliciting interest in a commercial device for making moulds of the reader's willy. At the magazine's twentieth birthday party Chris Donald gave due praise to discoverer–publisher, the suave John Brown. There were polite murmurs and a chaste ripple of applause. And then another member of the editorial team said really rather loudly, 'Oh yeah. And one last thing. John Brown. He's a posh twat.' Eruption of laughter. Relief. *Viz* offers its readers a distinctive view of the world. The Westminster-educated Brown later explained to me, 'Comedy comes from shit-holes. There are no comedians in Belgravia.' That in itself is a great British comic observation.

Victoria Wood
Arnold Brown

In 2001, Victoria Wood's farewell national tour culminated in ten sell-out nights of her show *Victoria Wood – At It Again* at the Royal Albert Hall, an appropriate setting for Britain's 'Queen of Stand-up Comedy'. Over the years, she had managed to fill this vast 5,000-seat venue for fifteen nights not once but twice. Only Billy Connolly and Ken Dodd have come anywhere near this level of popularity.

In her usual beguiling, breezy manner, she worked her magic on the audiences with surreal flights of fancy, dissecting without mercy all the minutiae of domestic life. This was vintage Wood – the national treasure the fans had known, cherished and loved since the early 1980s. However, this time she also spoke of her newer preoccupations, somewhat darker in tone than in previous performances. Now she had reached middle age there were the inevitable pressures of PMT, the menopause and raging hormones. And then there were her reflections, fuelled by some joyous celebrity-bashing, on the eating disorder for which she revealed she had had therapy. Most dramatically of all, she described in graphic detail the life-saving hysterectomy she had undergone earlier that year. The language used here had a new raunchy confidence, perhaps reflecting Victoria Wood's expressed desire to move on from familiar territory. She herself said that these final performances were the most self-revealing she has ever given on stage. Never before had she spoken directly to women while at the same time confronting her male audiences with raw insights into the most intimate problems faced by their wives, partners and lovers.

The art of stand-up comedy has always been – and still is – a male-dominated preserve. These final Albert Hall performances will remain a lasting testament to the remarkable fact that, with perhaps the exception of Jo Brand, Victoria Wood is the only female who has managed to break through this gender barrier on a national level. Even more extraordinary is the fact that such trail-blazing has been achieved without the benefit of role-models.

For all stand-ups, male and female alike, the need, and very often the compulsion, comedically to striptease one's inner personality before crowds of complete strangers can often be traced back to a childhood containing some void or emptiness in it that was never resolved, or indeed acknowledged. Being the centre of such rapt attention on stage is some kind of compensation for early traumas. The sound of laughter and applause gives the performer the message they always wanted to hear but never did. Yes, you do deserve to be the centre of attention. Yes, you are loved.

Victoria Wood was born on 19 May 1953 in Prestwich, Lancashire, and grew up, she says, 'in a huge bungalow in the middle of a field with no one for miles around'. Her mother, a teacher, and her father, a frustrated entertainer and writer who ended up as an insurance broker, were very close and didn't seem to need friends, so visitors were few and far between. Although she had two sisters and a brother (she was the youngest), it was a strange, lonely childhood, during which she learned to play the piano and amuse herself watching television on her own. The impression is of a rather dysfunctional background where the mother, in particular, seemed a distant figure to her children, and Victoria recalls that the family rarely ate together after she was fifteen.

When she was six, however, she was taken to see a one-woman show given by Joyce Grenfell, the quintessential English revue artist, renowned for her sharply observed character monologues and bitter-sweet songs. This was to be a serendipitous event for Victoria, planting the seed of the idea that comedy could be both her forte and her saviour. From an early age she had been writing plays and songs, which she never showed to anyone. During grammar school she attended a youth theatre for some time, then went on to study Drama and Arts at Birmingham University, but was turned down for drama school.

A turning-point came when a BBC producer spotted her playing her own songs at a party, and this led to the odd spot on Midlands TV magazine programmes, turning out ditties on various subjects, such as money, food or fashion. All this would later prove an invaluable apprenticeship for finding her own style and topics. When Victoria was twenty, she first came to the public's attention with success on the TV talent show *New Faces*, followed by appearances on Esther Rantzen's *That's Life*.

While she was working with cult comedian John Dowie she was invited to be in a revue, *In at the Death*, at London's small, but influential Bush Theatre. One of the other performers was a little-known actress called Julie Walters. Victoria went on to write a play entitled *Talent*, staged in 1978 at the Crucible Theatre, Sheffield, where she also appeared in a late-night show, *Funny Turns*, with Geoffrey Durham, a magician known as 'The Great Soprendo'. Both of these productions later came to London.

In 1979 she wrote a musical play, *Good Fun*, which included the song 'I've Had It up to Here with Men' wryly cataloguing past sexual encounters and wistfully concluding it would perhaps be more satisfactory to 'go from the foreplay straight to the cigarette'. The song proved a staple part of her act for some years afterwards, embodying as it did an eloquent cry from the heart with which countless women could identify. This vitriolic venting of frustration became the template for many of Victoria Wood's later targets. At long last someone was saying it exactly the way it was for the sisters. A later, more optimistic ballad on a related theme, 'Let's Do It', recounted the touching story of Freda and Barry and their strenuous efforts to achieve sexual nirvana, including the memorable exhortation: 'Beat me on the bottom with a *Woman's Weekly*.'

After a few years of touring with Geoffrey Durham, to whom she was now married, they made the decision to work separately. Her first major full-length show, *Lucky Bag*, opened at the King's Head in Islington in October 1983 and had more songs than stand-up or monologues, a ratio which was to be reversed in later years. The show had some Joyce Grenfell-like character pieces, including one where a pompous sixth-former makes an impassioned debate speech in defence of school uniforms. ('If you care to look at the Bayeux Tapestry... you will see that nearly everyone on that tapestry is wearing uniform'). Other pieces were a barbed surreal critique of

As seen on TV: Victoria Wood in 2001

geriatric Morecambe – 'where you can get a kiss-me-quick hearing aid' – and a plaintive song about a dull early marriage: 'it was the thing to do'.

Without the support of any such 'movement' as 'alternative comedy', Victoria Wood was already establishing herself as the first important stand-up comedienne in modern British comedy. In doing so, she was joining the ranks of her male peers, such as Billy Connolly, Dave Allen and Jasper Carrott. This in itself was undoubtedly a towering achievement, but at the same time she was also single-handedly writing her first television series. The result was six half-hour sketch shows called *Wood and Walters*, transmitted in 1982. The material was fresh, funny and original, with a rich diversity of comic characters – frigid cosmetic saleswomen in white coats, girls exchanging confidences, deranged shoe shop assistants, groupies, surburbanites mystified by 'Women's Lib', a cleaner subverting a snooty piano student's class-ridden assumptions. In all the two-handers, Victoria was invariably cast as the hapless target of a malevolent Julie Walters. These ping-pong exchanges are razor sharp, leaving the observant viewer in no doubt that this double act delighted in playing opposite each other.

Victoria Wood was by now one of the few women working in TV to have complete creative control over her work. This is specially reflected in the immaculate casting of a gifted repertory company of artists, such as Celia Imrie, Jim Broadbent, Duncan Preston and of course Julie Walters herself, who were gathered together to star in a second TV series, *Victoria Wood – As Seen on TV*, in 1985 on BBC2 (with an additional series of six in 1986). The quality of the sketches was as good as ever and included the still talked-about, heart-rending story of the unloved teenage Channel swimmer. There were also new characters, such as the intensely chatty continuity announcer, played by Susie Blake, and a weekly monologue from the outspoken Kitty from Manchester (Patricia Routledge), a monster from the provinces with her absurd confidences: 'I do have to be careful about my health because I have a grumbling ovary, which once flared up in the middle of *The Gondoliers*.' This type of observation, with its surprising turn of phrase and distinctive speech pattern, typified Victoria Wood's masterly command of the earthy language of ordinary Northern folk. There are obvious parallels here with Alan Bennett. And then, of course, there was 'Acorn Antiques', the triumphant parody of a TV soap opera, with Mrs Overall, Babs, Bertha, Clifford *et al*. Occasionally ending up in ensemble 'corpsing', this was as side-splitting as anything that Victoria Wood has ever done on TV.

Subsequently she went on to do a number of Christmas TV Specials, *An Audience with Victoria Wood*, the full-length TV film *Pat and Margaret* and lastly, starting in 1998, two series of *Dinnerladies*. Her prodigious output has been recognised by many awards, including a clutch of BAFTAS, a Doctor of Letters from Manchester University and in 1997 an OBE.

After her 2001 tour, she announced that she was fairly certain these would be her last live performances. 'I've gone as far as I want to do, talking about myself,' she said. '… I've got things in me that can't necessarily be encapsulated in stand-up.' Her very special presence on the big stage will be sadly missed by her legions of fans, but they can take comfort from the fact that she relinquished her crown while at the top of her game. She has talked of concentrating on writing films in future.

In the meantime, Victoria, from all of us, thank you for everything.

Yes Minister
Roy Hattersley

For politicians of my generation – Harold Wilson's government and Jim Callaghan's cabinet – *Yes Minister* was more than a classic comedy. Indeed, we sometimes wondered if it was a comedy at all. For while other viewers recognised it instantly as a brilliant satire, we saw it as an only slightly distorted representation of our daily lives. I suspect that a new generation of parliamentary secretaries and secretaries of state feel much the same. Twenty years after the original series was broadcast, I watched an episode on one of those late-night channels which specialise in what they call vintage television. Jim Hacker, Minister for Administrative Affairs, was arguing with his 'special adviser' about patronage. Too many jobs, the apparatchik said, were going to 'cronies' or were being used as inducements for favours. Were we, I wondered, really accused of that back in the Seventies? Or did Anthony Jay and Jonathan Lynn anticipate the scandals of the Nineties as accurately as they portrayed the absurdities of an earlier generation?

Of course, both *Yes Minister* and *Yes Prime Minister* reflected life in Westminster and Whitehall through a distorting mirror. But from day one the image they screened was always a recognisable caricature of the real thing. After the 1966 and 1974 general elections, when the new governments were being formed, I waited anxiously beside the telephone in exactly the way Jim Hacker waited for his call to greatness. Like him, I was infuriated by friends who announced, 'Just phoned to find out if you've heard anything yet'. Our fury had the same two distinct causes – hopes dashed by the discovery that it was not Downing Street on the line, and fear that Number 10 had dialled my number and found it engaged. I have spent many anxious hours imagining prime ministers saying, 'If he's not keen enough to keep his line clear for my call, he's not keen enough to serve in my administration'.

For me, the cabinet call came in the summer of 1976 and produced a farce which was well worthy of *Yes Minister*. I saw the Prime Minister at eleven in the morning and he told me that my appointment would be announced at three o'clock that afternoon. Until then, I had to tell nobody. Of course, I rushed home with the good news. Three o'clock passed without the announcement being made. So did four and five. By six I was on the train to Birmingham to fulfil an unbreakable constituency engagement. When I arrived at New Street the stationmaster was waiting for me. I was, he said in appropriately urgent tones, to telephone Downing Street at once. This, I thought, was it. Because I had broken silence, my promotion had been cancelled. Twice I dialled the wrong number. When I got through, the Private Secretary was as apologetic as only senior civil servants can be. Neil Kinnock had declined to become my parliamentary secretary. Finding a replacement had caused the delay. If that had happened to Jim Hacker, heads would have been shaken in a thousand sitting rooms: 'Couldn't possibly be true.'

I turned up at my new office, just as Jim Hacker turned up at his, with a political adviser in tow. In both cases the appendage was brought in to demonstrate, right from the start, that the minister intended to be guided more by the policy and philosophy of his party than by the cynical pragmatism of the civil service. For both Hacker and me, it was the beginning of a wrestling match in which what we thought was right competed with what they thought was possible. The difference between life and art was that my civil servants opposed my ideas openly, whereas the officials of the Department of Administrative Affairs worked in devious ways. My permanent secretary, Sir Kenneth Clucas, was just as clever as Sir Humphrey Appleby and held his opinions just as strongly. But he always attempted to impose his will on mine by force of argument. When I overruled him and was proved wrong, he never once said, 'I told you so'. He may have discussed my faults with other permanent secretaries and plotted with them to overthrow me, but I doubt it.

Plain dealing was a feature of the domestic departments. In the Ministry of Defence (where I was called Minister for Defence (Administration) long before Jim Hacker expropriated the abstract noun) and the Foreign Office (where I was Minister of State) life was much less straightforward. Part of Sir Humphrey's secret was not allowing his minister to realise that the political decisions had been stalled or sidetracked. So perhaps I should not have been surprised that I had been duped for so long when, a quarter of a century after the event, I discovered that it had happened to me.

In 1974, the Foreign Secretary asked me to consider if it was possible for Britain to adopt a 'more positive' – that is to say, less aggressive – policy towards the Soviet Union and its satellites. After much argument with the diplomats, I submitted (as requested) a policy paper. Jim Callaghan signified his 'general approval' and said that he would have further meetings about the implementation of my ideas. We both then moved on – he to the premiership and I to the cabinet. I did not even think about my small contribution to *glasnost* until the Foreign Office documents for the period were published twenty-five years later. Among them was an angry telegram from our ambassador in Moscow. A new policy on Eastern Europe had been agreed. Why had he not been told about it? The answer from the Foreign Office would have been insufficiently subtle for Sir Humphrey, but he would have admired its message. The 'new policy' had only been agreed by ministers. Officials had still to decide whether or not to implement it!

The problem with the Ministry of Defence was that it always wanted more money and was willing to do almost anything to get it. In one celebrated episode of *Yes Prime Minister* the rescue of a lost dog on Salisbury Plain – welcomed by a delighted Prime Minister Hacker because of the favourable publicity it would generate – was subsequently used as a lever by which the government could be forced into increasing the military budget. I was sandbagged in more harrowing circumstances and with the help of a less cuddly animal. On a visit to the Ghurkhas in Nepal during the New Year of 1970 I was

'Yes Prime Minister': Paul Eddington as Jim Hacker and Nigel Hawthorne as Sir Humphrey Appleby

flown high in the Himalayas to an army hospital. Usually such visits are confined to brief meetings with happy convalescents. In Nepal that year I was shown every possible horror – including a local woman whose face had recently been half-removed by a bear. My distress at the sight provoked the enquiry, why was I being harrowed in this way? The response, although itself a question, provided a very clear answer. Did I want the hospital to go on treating Ghurkha families and, if so, would I find the money for extra staff?

Like Hacker, I lived in constant fear that my failures would be found out and I would be summarily returned to the backbenches. In the end, it was the electorate rather than the Prime Minister who removed me from office – by far the lesser of the two indignities. But I remained in a state of permanent anxiety. In perfect Hacker fashion, I always assumed that I would be blamed for whatever went wrong. I recall one cabinet meeting when the Prime Minister announced his firm intention of dismissing whoever was responsible for a particularly damaging leak. Innocent though I was, I was sure that he suspected me. Indeed, as he warmed to his subject I began to believe that it *was* me. I think my nerve was undermined by the fact that the story had been written in a newspaper for which I once worked by a journalist who was a friend of mine.

Hacker was not a great success at media manipulation. Neither was I. But at least I never made a promise, in front of television cameras, without the slightest thought of whether or not it could be kept and (more important) whether I would be found out. Hacker's greatest error – guaranteeing the future of a city farm when, it later transpired, his own department had authorised office building on the site – followed the unnerving experience of being brushed aside by a swarm of children in pursuit of Sue Lawley's autograph. I got used to that sort of thing. Over a couple of years I met at London Airport Henry Kissinger, Archbishop Makarios, Pierre Trudeau, Helmut Schmidt and numerous other international celebrities. I was always trampled underfoot by photographers who wanted their pictures but not mine. Fortunately I was always too traumatised by the experience to say anything immediately afterwards – damaging or not.

But I did identify with Hacker whenever his private secretary appeared – particularly when comparisons were made between Oxford and other universities, and Latin tags were first quoted and then translated into English. My private secretaries went on to great glories – assistant secretary general of the United Nations and then warden of St Antony's College, Oxford; the Queen's press secretary; the chairman and chief executive of the John Lewis Partnership; and the electricity regulator, the man who decides how much it costs to switch on the lights. Poor Bernard never progressed beyond the private office. But he managed to exude an intellectual superiority which I instantly recognised. And that was, of course, the irresistible subtext of *Yes Minister*. The politician, although titular boss, occupies a lower position in the pack order. Is that also true to life? It is all too long ago for me to remember.

The Young Ones
Nick Groom

In retrospect, it all seems so simple: a sitcom based in a dilapidated student house, showcasing upcoming young comedians. But that's hardly recognisable as *The Young Ones* – which most people remember by the noisome exploits of its principal characters. They lived in ridiculous squalour, ate only lentils, made embarrassingly puerile jokes (in ironic postmodern fashion, of course), smashed up everything, and spent a lot of time shouting 'You utter, utter bastard' at each other.

The Young Ones is a sitcom, but a punked-up, magic-realist sitcom. Completely grotesque yet painfully accurate, it is a monstrous parody of students and the student lifestyle – and don't anyone dare say that they live 'just like the Young Ones', unless whenever they are about to have a party their houses are half-demolished by gigantic ham sandwiches discarded by the Four Horsemen of the Apocalypse. Nevertheless, the four undergraduates are all embarrassingly familiar characters. Rik (Rik Mayall) reckons he's a 'right on' anarchist and the people's poet – in fact, he's a sanctimonious and self-centred little prig with the emotional maturity of a sniggering thirteen-year-old; Vyvyan (Adrian Edmondson) is a psychopathic, headbanging medical student, who sports a row of studs in his forehead and keeps a Glaswegian hamster called SPG (Special Patrol Group); Neil (Nigel Planer) is the fall guy, a miserable hippie always shuffling around and complaining about how 'heavy' everything is; and Mike (Christopher Ryan) is a midget conman evidently blackmailing the university's vice-chancellor and living in a fantasy world of cool in which he effortlessly hobnobs with celebrities and sex kittens.

Together, these four explosively incompatible housemates barely do anything but bicker and fight about the most excruciatingly mundane things – paying the bills, going to the laundrette, borrowing a coin for the phone, answering the door. It is positively Beckettian in its banality – except that around this black hole of mindless boredom and acute pettiness revolves a mad universe of the strangest and most inexplicable events. Their whole hallucinatory world is teemingly alive: the fruit in the fridge makes cheap sexual innuendoes, the toilet eats bog-brushes, one of Vyvyan's socks escapes and has to be beaten to death with a frying pan. The weirdest people come and go: members of the Balowski family (landlord, party drunk, international arms dealer, medieval jester – all played by Alexei Sayle); two shipwrecked men who are holidaying on a raft under a lightbulb in the cellar; Cinderella, who stays at their party past midnight and promptly turns into a pumpkin; the ghosts of two decapitated Elizabethans, who get their heads mixed up; a premature Easter Bunny; and a teapot genie, who gives Neil six pairs of arms. 'The nuttiest things happen in this crazy house', as Rik puts it at one point, aping a

---

Overleaf: Rik Mayall, Christopher Ryan, Nigel Planer and Adrian Edmondson as the Young Ones.

cretinously zany commentator: an unexploded atom bomb lands in front of the fridge, the lads discover that their wardrobe leads to the magical kingdom of Narnia, they appear on *University Challenge* against Footlights College, Oxbridge (despite Vyv losing his head on the way there when he oh-so-rebelliously leans out of the train window), and the whole house is transported back to the Middle Ages.

Noisy, stupid, fantastically odd, and still unbelievably funny, *The Young Ones* was the 'alternative' comedy scene's rambunctious coming of age. Most of the performers came out of London's Comedy Store club, which was compèred by Sayle, and later by Ben Elton, and gave a platform to a new breed of aspiring, radical and subversive comedians. Mayall and Edmondson, for example, originally developed their ultra-violent slapstick, which features heavily in the show, as the Comedy Store's 'Dangerous Brothers'. But until *The Young Ones,* there had been hardly any television exposure of this edgy new comedy.

They tackled the new medium by deconstructing the whole concept of that TV standby, the sitcom. Mayall and Lise Mayer wrote the scripts, Elton pulled their stream-of-consciousness into shape, and they managed to combine situation comedy with the cabaret format of the Comedy Store, thereby introducing dozens of new comedians to the nation. But at the same time they created something that was so knowing, so self-aware and so self-mocking that it actually ridiculed humour itself. You laugh at the gags, you laugh (again, of course, in ironic postmodern fashion) at the laboured jokes which mock the imbecility of mainstream comedy, and you laugh at the scathing satires of traditional sitcoms: ultimately, you laugh at the whole idea of people laughing at anything at all. It's dizzying.

The post-punk generation needed to rebel against the old folks with something more than music and fashion, and *The Young Ones* did feel, if only for a few months, like the new rock'n'roll – not least because the show's entirely spurious musical slot featured happening bands like Madness and Motörhead. The Goons, the Pythons, even *The Goodies* may have been as out of control as *The Young Ones*, but by the 1980s they were all firmly Establishment: the grand old tradition of anarchic British humour. Everyone from your father to Prince Charles told you to listen to the *Goon Show, Python* was a very English institution one followed with an awed and often baffled admiration, and parents, grandparents, and aunts and uncles would merrily endorse comedy from *Fawlty Towers* to Benny Hill. Yes, they were funny, but we young ones needed our own comedy – and *The Young Ones* was just that. Obsessed with zits, crapping and wanking, like the evergreen comic *Viz* it was in-your-face rude – which is precisely why our parents never got it.

Talking of parents, the hippie Neil Pye's mum and dad once managed to visit him and his housemates, arriving in the middle of a street riot during which some joker has impaled a head to their front door. The episode ('Sick') is typical. All the characters – from the Young Ones themselves to the blazers-and-British-Legion Mr and Mrs Pye to a police officer who arrives simply to hit Rik with a chair – cheerfully admit that this is just a TV show.

Neil's Mum: You have brought shame on your family, Neil. I daren't show my face at Lady Fanshaw's bridge evenings, now that you've taken up with these television people. I mean, what kind of monsters are you? I mean, *The Young Ones*. Well, it all sounds very good, doesn't it? But just look around you. It's trash! [She smashes a chair.] I mean… even *Triangle* has better furniture than you do!

Mike: I think you'll find that was specially designed to fall apart like that, Mrs Pye. Rik was going to get hit over the head with it in the next scene.

This out-of-telly experience then continues with a sharp parody of *Grange Hill*, before the opening sequence of *The Good Life* rolls. Vyvyan spectacularly tears down the screen, declaring, 'No! No! No! We're not watching the bloody *Good Life*! Bloody, bloody, bloody! I hate it! It's so bloody *nice*! Felicity "Treacle" Kendal and Richard "Sugar-flavoured-snot" Briers! …They're just a couple of reactionary stereotypes, confirming the myth that everyone in Britain is a lovable, middle-class eccentric – and I HATE THEM!' Rik, self-deluding anarchist and card-carrying Cliff Richard fan that he is, returns us to TV-land, declaring his love for Ms Kendal. The storyline then digresses into a cross between *Macbeth* and *The Good Life*, in which Rik accidentally kills Neil. Rik hides the body in manure, and is tortured all night by the voice of his conscience (which is so loud it keeps Vyvyan awake), before Neil returns from the grave – or rather Neils do: under the compost, Neil has germinated like a seed and grown into three. As the Neils greet the terrified Rik, the entire set suddenly disappears to reveal Neil's parents and Brian Damage, 'a violent and highly dangerous escaped criminal madman', waving and blowing kisses to the studio audience from a glitzy stage while a continuity announcer declares, 'Good evening, and welcome to *Nice Time*'. The Young Ones themselves frantically jump up and down flashing V-signs and trying to get into shot as the credits roll. Evidently nothing makes sense once your parents arrive.

It is not simply surreal, it is purely bizarre. And there's another element that makes this so great, so British, and so funny: embarrassment. Embarrassment has always been a key feature of British comedy, and *The Young Ones* surely takes it as far as it can go. Neil's parents coming to tea is embarrassing enough, but who can forget Rik's party, where he forbids everyone to drink before the party starts, sucks up to his trendy sociology tutor like a total bloody swot, and thinks that a tampon is a carefully wrapped present – a mouse hiding in a telescope? Or Rik's pretend girlfriend: having woken up in bed with a girlie, he gives a blow-by-blow account of their night's adventures to his male housemates (which Mike records on tape), before she appears and reveals that the entire encounter is entirely fictitious. Rik is condemned to wear a sign around his neck reading 'I am a Virgin'.

I still cringe, even as I laugh. *The Young Ones* is less the successor to *George and Mildred* than the bastard love-child of Samuel Beckett and Alan Bennett. It is wild comedy based on endless and obsessive non-sequiturs and cataclysmic moments of fatal misunderstanding which generate their own crazy logic. Stupid is funny and, in this case, very stupid is absolutely bloody hilarious.

Biographies

Nigel Andrews

Nigel Andrews has been film critic of the *Financial Times* for thirty years and a regular contributor to BBC radio as a reviewer and writer–presenter. He has written four books: *Horror Movies*, *True Myths: The Life and Times of Arnold Schwarzenegger*, *Travolta the Life*, and *Jaws*. Twice named Critic of the Year in the British Press Awards (1985, 2002), he is a Fellow of the Royal Society of Arts.

Stephen Bayley

Stephen Bayley is a design consultant, author and ocean-going commentator. His Boilerhouse Project at the V&A was London's most popular gallery of the 1980s and the Design Museum that evolved from it a world first. His books include *In Good Shape*; *Sex, Drink and Fast Cars*; *Taste*; *Harley Earl*; and *Sex*. In 1989 he was made a Chevalier de l'Ordre des Arts et Lettres by the French Minister of Culture.

Tony Booth

Tony Booth has been an actor for forty years, and is best known for his role as Mike, Alf Garnett's left-wing son-in-law in the long-running comedy series *Till Death Us Do Part*. He contributed sketches to *That Was the Week That Was* and has published a volume of memoirs, *What's Left?*

Arnold Brown

The first stand-up comedian to win the prestigious Perrier Award in 1987, Arnold Brown was one of the founder members of the Comedy Store and Comic Strip in the early 1980s. He is a frequent BBC contributor and has written a comic novella *Are You Looking at Me, Jimmy?*

Craig Brown

Craig Brown writes the 'Way of the World' column three times a week for the *Daily Telegraph*, a weekly book review for the *Mail on Sunday* and the parodic Diary in *Private Eye*. His books include *A Year Inside*, a selection of his *Times* parliamentary sketches, *The Marsh Marlowe Letters*, *The Hounding of John Thomas*, *The Agreeable World of Wallace Arnold* and, most recently, *This Is Craig Brown*.

Michael Bywater

Michael Bywater writes for a variety of newspapers and journals, including the *Independent on Sunday*, the *Observer* and the *New Statesman*. A long-time friend and collaborator of Douglas Adams, he worked with him on several projects, including the computer game *Starship Titanic*.

Joseph Connolly

Joseph Connolly worked in publishing and was an antiquarian bookseller before becoming a full-time writer. He is the author of eight novels published by Faber & Faber, as well as of many non-fiction works. He has written for a wide range of newspapers and magazines, most notably *The Times*.

Ray Connolly

Ray Connolly is best known for his journalism, which is currently being published in the *Daily Mail*. As well as several novels and radio plays, he has written screenplays (including *That'll Be the Day* and *Stardust*), TV series (*Lytton's Diary* and *Perfect Scoundrels*), TV documentaries and a biography of John Lennon.

Michael Coveney

Michael Coveney is the theatre critic of the *Daily Mail*, having served in that same post on the *Financial Times* and the *Observer*. His books include a history of the Glasgow Citizens Theatre and critical biographies of actress Maggie Smith, filmmaker Mike Leigh and composer Andrew Lloyd Webber.

Barry Cryer

Barry Cryer worked with Tommy Cooper on Thames Television and London Weekend Television, but he's feeling better now. Tommy became a friend as well as a colleague and delighted him with his consistent inconsistency. Barry Cryer now tours with his own show, *The First Farewell Tour*, and speaks after dinner around the country, ever in search of a free meal. Since 1972 he has been appearing in Radio 4's *I'm Sorry I Haven't a Clue*. Comic, writer, actor and composer, he says he is not versatile, just confused.

Christopher Dunkley

Christopher Dunkley is a freelance critic and commentator on the mass media, working chiefly in newspapers and on the radio. He was for thirty years television critic of the *Financial Times*, where he was twice named Critic of the Year in the British Press Awards, and for thirteen years presenter of *Feedback* on Radio 4.

Fergus Fleming

Fergus Fleming worked in publishing for six years before becoming a full-time writer in 1991. His books include *Barrow's Boys*, *Killing Dragons*, *Ninety Degrees North*, and *The Sword and the Cross*. He has also written a number of non-fiction titles for younger readers, among them Usborne's cult *Newspaper Histories* (in collaboration with Paul Dowswell). His current project is *Cassell's Tales of Endurance*.

Sue Gaisford

Sue Gaisford is a freelance journalist, writer and broadcaster. She has written about radio for the *Radio Times* and for the *Independent on Sunday*. She lives with her family in Sussex.

Suzi Godson

Suzi Godson is author and designer of the award-winning *Sex Book*. For the past two years she has written a weekly column called 'S is for Sex' in the *Independent on Sunday* and she has written features on sex, health, lifestyle, relationships, teenage issues and child health for, among others, the *Independent*, the *Observer*, *Marie Claire*, *Elle* and *Cosmopolitan*. Her books include *Women Unlimited*, *The Directory for Life* and the children's cookbook *Eat Up*.

Jonathon Green

Jonathon Green is Britain's leading lexicographer of slang. Among his most recent books are the *Cassell Dictionary of Slang* (1998), the *Macmillan Dictionary of Contemporary Slang* (1996) and *Slang down the Ages: the Historical Development of Slang* (1993). His history of lexicography, *Chasing the Sun: Dictionary-makers and the Dictionaries They Made*, appeared in 1996. His current project is the multi-volumed *Cassell Historical Dictionary of Slang*.

Sarah Gristwood

Sarah Gristwood is the author of *Arbella: England's Lost Queen*, and of an earlier book about the history of women's diaries. After leaving Oxford she worked for more than ten years as a freelance journalist, appearing in newspapers such as the *Guardian*, the *Daily Telegraph* and the *Evening Standard*. Specialising in film and television, she interviewed a long list of celebrities, including several members of the *Blackadder* team.

Nick Groom

Nick Groom lives on Dartmoor and teaches English at Bristol University. He has published articles on topics from muzak to erotica to the invention of fish 'n' chips, and is the author of *The Forger's Shadow: How Forgery Changed the Course of Literature* and, with the illustrator Piero, *Introducing Shakespeare*.

Janie Hampton

Janie Hampton has written fourteen books, including the first biography of Joyce Grenfell, and was a journalist for the BBC World Service in Zimbabwe, Kenya and the Congo. Her articles on travel have appeared in the *Daily Telegraph* and *Sunday Times* and her obituaries in the *Independent*. While raising four children, she also designed family planning programmes in Africa, South America and the South Pacific.

Adam Hart-Davis

Adam Hart-Davis collected a degree in chemistry at Oxford and a doctorate at York, then did three years' research, mainly in Western Canada. After five years in science publishing, he went in 1977 to Yorkshire Television, where for seventeen years he researched and produced science programmes before getting the wrong side of the camera by mistake. He is now a freelance photographer, writer, and broadcaster on radio and television.

Roy Hattersley

Roy Hattersley joined the Labour government as Under-secretary of State at the Department of Employment in 1967, and subsequently served as Minister of Defence, Senior Minister of State at the Foreign Office, and Secretary of State for Prices and Consumer Affairs. He became a Privy Councillor in 1975. Deputy Leader of the Labour Party from 1983 until 1992, he stood down from Parliament in 1997 to concentrate on writing and speaking, and was created Baron Hattersley of Sparkbrook in the dissolution honours. He is the author of sixteen books including a trilogy of novels, five books of essays and the classic autobiographical memoir *A Yorkshire Boyhood*. He contributes to numerous newspapers and magazines, radio and TV, and has been voted Granada Television's Columnist of the Year.

Simon Hoggart

Simon Hoggart is parliamentary sketchwriter for the *Guardian*, and chairman of Radio 4's *The News Quiz*. He was seventeen when *That Was the Week That Was* first appeared.

Chrissy Iley

Chrissy Iley has tried to measure her life in *Absolutely Fabulous* moments, and in the meantime has written for most national newspapers, most frequently the *Sunday Times* and the *Daily Mail*, and *Glamour*. She lives mostly in London and mostly to excess.

Oliver James

Oliver James worked as a clinical psychologist at the Cassel Hospital in South London for six years. Since 1982 he has produced or presented over thirty TV documentaries and written weekly columns for the *Sun*, the *Independent*, the *Sunday Telegraph*, the *Sunday Express* and, at present, the *Observer* Magazine. He is a trustee of Home-Start and of the National Family and Parenting Institute. He is the author of *They F*** You Up – How to Survive Family Life*; *Britain on the Couch – Why We're Unhappier Compared with 1950 Despite Being Richer*; and *Juvenile Violence in a Winner-Loser Culture*.

Iain Johnstone

Iain Johnstone devised BBC's Film 71, which he presented in 1983 and 1984. He was nominated as Best Director by the British Academy for *Snowdon on Camera*. After twelve years as Film Critic for the *Sunday Times*, he joined John Cleese to write *Fierce Creatures* and has just completed *The Bank of San Bernadino* and a series of four documentaries for Steven Spielberg.

Mark Lewisohn

Mark Lewisohn is the author of the definitive encyclopedia of television humour, *Radio Times Guide to TV Comedy*, and the acclaimed biography of Benny Hill, *Funny, Peculiar*. A contributor to *Radio Times* since 1990, he specialises in the history, recent and distant, of radio and TV broadcasting. A leading authority on The Beatles, he is the author of a range of celebrated reference books, including *The Complete Beatles Recording Sessions* and *The Complete Beatles Chronicle*, and is currently writing his first full biography of the group.

Bob McCabe

Bob McCabe is well known as a film critic and author of over a dozen film-related books, including the bestselling *Dark Knights and Holy Fools: The Art and Films of Terry Gilliam*; *The Exorcist: Out of the Shadows*; and *Ronnie Barker: The Authorised Biography*. He has recently helped several former Pythons put together *Monty Python*'s official autobiography.

Graham McCann

Graham McCann has written a number of books on comedy and comic actors, including *Morecambe and Wise* and *Dad's Army*. He also contributes regularly on politics and culture to a wide range of publications.

Annabel Merullo

Annabel Merullo has spent her career working in television and book publishing. She is the co-creator of the successful series of Century books, including *The Russian Century*, *The British Century* and *The Chinese Century*. She has recently edited an anthology of war reportage entitled *The Eye of War*, with an introduction by John Keegan. She was also the co-editor of *British Greats* and *British Sporting Greats*.

Stephen Moss

Stephen Moss is a staff writer on the *Guardian*, for which he has written on TV, film, books, music and sport.

James Naughtie

James Naughtie presents the *Today* programme on BBC Radio 4. He also introduces music on BBC radio and television and is the host of Radio 4's *Bookclub*. He is a former chief political correspondent of the *Guardian* and the *Scotsman*, and writes for many newspapers and magazines.

Robin Oakley

Robin Oakley has been writing about and broadcasting on politics since the 1970s. He has been Crossbencher on the *Sunday Express*, an assistant editor of the *Daily Mail* and Political Editor of *The Times* and of the BBC. He is now European Political Editor for CNN. He also contributes a regular column on horseracing to the